Mappings of the Plane

GWEN HARWOOD was born in 192\
up in Brisbane, where she complete
marriage in 1945 she moved to Hoba
an academic position, and where she
Ludwig Wittgenstein. Her first col\
produced poems under several other r.
to poetry, wrote a number of opera libretti. Harwood's anti-authoritarian
wit was displayed in prose in her letters. She died in 1995.

GREGORY KRATZMANN, formerly Associate Professor of English at La
Trobe University, is the editor of *A Steady Storm of Correspondence:
Selected Letters of Gwen Harwood 1943–1995* (2001) and with Alison
Hoddinott, *Gwen Harwood: Collected Poems 1943–1995* (2003), both
published by the University of Queensland Press. He has written exten-
sively in the areas of Australian literature and English medieval literature.

CHRIS WALLACE-CRABBE is Professor Emeritus in the Australian Centre,
the University of Melbourne. His first book of poems was published in
Australia in 1959. His most recent books of verse include *By and Large*
(Carcanet, 2001), *The Universe Looks Down* (Brandl and Schlesinger, 2005)
and *Telling a Hawk from a Handsaw* (Carcanet, 2008). Chris Wallace-
Crabbe chairs the newly established Australian Poetry Centre in St Kilda,
Victoria. Among other awards, he has won the Dublin Prize for Arts and
Sciences and the Christopher Brennan Award for Literature.

Fyfield*Books* aim to make available some of the classics of world literature in clear, affordable formats, and to restore often neglected writers to their place in literary tradition.

Fyfield*Books* take their name from the Fyfield elm in Matthew Arnold's 'Scholar Gypsy' and 'Thyrsis'. The tree stood not far from the village where the series was originally devised in 1971.

> *Roam on! The light we sought is shining still.*
> *Dost thou ask proof? Our tree yet crowns the hill,*
> *Our Scholar travels yet the loved hill-side*

from 'Thyrsis'

GWEN HARWOOD

Mappings of the Plane
NEW SELECTED POEMS

Edited with an introduction by
GREGORY KRATZMANN
and
CHRIS WALLACE-CRABBE

FyfieldBooks
CARCANET

First published in Great Britain in 2009 by
Carcanet Press Limited
Alliance House
Cross Street
Manchester M2 7AQ

The publisher acknowledges financial assistance from Arts Council England

Typeset by XL Publishing Services, Tiverton
Printed and bound in England by SRP Ltd, Exeter

To the memory of Thomas Riddell

Contents

from *The Lion's Bride* (1981)

from *Bone Scan* (1988)

from *The Present Tense* (1995)

from *Collected Poems 1943–1995*
(Formerly uncollected poems)

Two poems by Alan Carvosso (Uncollected)

Introduction

Gwen Harwood has been described by Peter Porter, in a review of her *Collected Poems, 1943-1995* as 'the outstanding Australian poet of the twentieth century', a view that has long been shared by other readers. Her poetry is remarkable at many levels: for its range, its wit, and its humane intelligence. Whether the poems are written in formal metres and structures, or whether constructed in freer forms, they offer delight at the primal levels of their musicality and their ability to shift the boundaries between the verbal and the oral. There is no other voice in English-language poetry that resembles hers, and her dominant tone was established very early in her publishing career, along with her formal versatility. A self-proclaimed 'capital-R Romantic', Harwood's affiliations are with European traditions – not only literary, but also musical and philosophical, although her work displays a keen eye for the Australian landscape and a keen ear for vernacular idiom. (As Fleur Adcock pointed out in another review, the rhyme of 'wattle' with 'Aristotle' is unique in English-language poetry.)

Gwen Harwood was born Gwendoline Foster in 1920 in subtropical Brisbane, where she studied piano and composition, and played the organ at All Saints', Brisbane's foremost Anglo-Catholic church. From time to time attempts have been made to claim her as a religious poet, but this is true only in the sense defined in her late poem 'A Scattering of Ashes' – 'Music, my joy, my full-scale God'.

She married the academic F.W. (Bill) Harwood at the end of the war, and they moved to Hobart in Tasmania; the effect of the change from sunny sprawling Brisbane to the chilly English beauty of Australia's southernmost city is recalled in '1945', included in this selection. The Harwoods had four children in the years to 1952, and she lived the life of a busy housewife and mother. Gwen Harwood did not publish a volume of poetry until she was forty-three, but she did write many poems for journals and little magazines. 'The Dead Gums' and 'Water-Music', two poems from 1949 which already illustrate her lyrical mastery and her eye for the arresting image, are included here.

When she died in 1995, Gwen Harwood had published six major collections of poetry at intervals of approximately six years: *Poems* (1963) was followed by *Poems/Volume Two* (1968), *Selected Poems* (1975), *The Lion's Bride* (1981), *Bone Scan* (1988), and *The Present Tense* (1995). She was a rigorous self-editor, and the result of this was that many fine poems published in sometimes obscure and short-lived Australian magazines disappeared from view. A Harwood 'canon', shaped by the successive editions of her *Selected Poems*, came into being, and after her death her editors Alison Hoddinott and Gregory Kratzmann decided that it was time to reinstate the many poems which had fallen into the netherworld of 'Uncollected'. *Collected Poems, 1943-1995*, published by University of Queensland Press in 2003, gives access to almost all of her poetic *œuvre*. The *Collected* is the basis of the present edition, and the utmost care has been taken to preserve the poet's care for the shape of her lines on the page, manifest in indenting, spaces within lines, and the running of sentences across divisions of stanza and line.

One curious product of Gwen Harwood's editing of her own work for the various Australian texts of her *Selected Poems* which appeared during her lifetime was the removal of the original pseudonymous signatures attached to some of her most memorable work from the 1960s and early 70s. Works published originally by Walter Lehmann, Francis Geyer, and Miriam Stone appeared in time under her own name, thereby obscuring one of the most fascinating phenomena in the history of twentieth-century poetry publishing. Gwen Harwood made newspaper headlines in 1961 when it became known that she was the 'Walter Lehmann' who had written two sonnets published in *The Bulletin*, then one of Australia's most important forums for new writing. 'Eloisa to Abelard' and 'Abelard to Eloisa' created a brief furore when it became known that they contained acrostic messages, one containing the word which had been largely responsible for the banning in Australia of Lawrence's *Lady Chatterley's Lover*.

Walter Lehmann was also the author of 'In the Park', that keen-edged vignette of motherhood for which Gwen Harwood continues to be remembered in anthologies. Francis Geyer, exiled Hungarian music-lover and poet, is represented here by 'At the Arts Club' and 'Ebb-Tide', and Miriam Stone (Harwood's only female pseudonym) by 'Burning Sappho', with the last two lines of the third stanza restored to their original lacerating version. A fourth poet-self, Timothy Kline, who speaks for the 'generation of 1968', was suppressed completely by his creator, but here he speaks again in 'Poet and Peasant', 'Frog Prince' and 'Emporium'. A fifth Harwood pseudonym came to light some years after her death and the publication of *Collected Poems*. Alan Carvosso is the author of two poems inspired by music, 'O Sleep, why dost thou leave me?' and 'On Wings of Song', published here as parts of a Harwood *Selected Poems* for the first time.

Her fondness for 'masques, masquerades, wigs and beards', evident in the creation of poet-selves, also finds expression in her creation of poetic 'characters', the nuclear physicist Professor Eisenbart and the exiled

European pianist Professor Kröte: Eisenbart is represented here by 'Prize-Giving' and 'Boundary Conditions', Kröte by 'A Scattering of Ashes'.

Piercing, witty, passionate, reflective, as much an elegist as a trickster, Gwen Harwood wrote across a wide variety of forms and genres, including occasional poetry. Often she wrote 'Sappho cards' to friends. These are her distinctive contribution to the art of the verse letter, usually hand-made, featuring an etching from a Victorian ladies' magazine with speech balloons purloined from her children's comic books; one of them, ' "Wolfgang," said father Leopold' is included here.

Ironically, it was as a librettist rather than as a poet that she wished to be remembered, and only a small number of music specialists are familiar with her extraordinary talent for writing words for music. Over some thirty years she wrote libretti for the composer Larry Sitsky; although she claimed that the words belonged to the music, many of these texts retain extraordinary dramatic power for readers as well as listeners in the concert hall. The extent to which her practice in song-writing, where gaps have to be left for the music to fill out, influenced the freer forms of her later poetic texts has still to be fully appreciated.

Some of Gwen Harwood's most moving poems are addressed to friends, including several leading Australian poets, musicians, and artists. Her poems, like her letters (see *Blessed City*, edited by Alison Hoddinott, and *A Steady Storm of Correspondence: Selected Letters of Gwen Harwood 1943–1995*, edited by Gregory Kratzmann), celebrate the sustaining and redemptive power of friendship. Chief among her friends was the broadcaster, actor and singer Thomas ('Tony') Riddell, who first encouraged her to write, and who remained her confidant for more than fifty years. It is fitting that this edition, like all but one of her published volumes, should be dedicated to his memory.

Gregory Kratzmann
Chris Wallace-Crabbe
Melbourne, 2008

from *Poems*
(1963)

Alter Ego

Who stands beside me still,
nameless, indifferent
to any lost or ill
motion of mind or will,
whose pulse is mine, who goes
sleepless and is not spent?

Mozart said he could hear
a symphony complete,
its changing harmonies clear
plain in his inward ear
in time without extent.
And this one, whom I greet

yet cannot name, or see
save as light's sidelong shift,
who will not answer me,
knows what I was, will be,
and all I am: beyond
time's desolating drift.

In half-light I rehearse
Mozart's cascading thirds.
Light's lingering tones disperse.
Music and thought reverse
their flow. Beside dark roots
dry crickets call like birds

that morning when I came
from childhood's steady air
to love, like a blown flame,
and learned: time will reclaim
all music manifest.
Wait, then, beside my chair

as time and music flow
nightward again. I trace
their questioning voices, know
little, but learn, and go
on paths of love and pain
to meet you, face to face.

At the Water's Edge

To Vivian Smith

Smooth, reptilian, soaring,
a gull wheels away from this rock
leaving the scraps I was throwing,

and settles again in a flurry
of foam and plumed air. The wild seaweed
crawls crimson and green in my shadow.

The gull's flight aches in my shoulders.
It will suffer no change, cannot offer
itself to be changed, cannot suffer:

the forms born of earth are supported
by earth, body-sheltering, guileless.
'What is truth?' asks the heart, and is told:

> You will suffer, and gaze at the fact
> of the world until pain's after-image
> is as real as pain; all your strength
>
> will be fretted to grains of distress;
> you will speak to the world; what you offer
> will toss upon evil and good
>
> to be snatched or disdained. You will find
> all nature exhausted as beauty
> though radiant as mystery still.
>
> You will learn what was breathed into dust
> the sixth day, when the fowls of the air
> wheeled over your flightless dominion.

'What is truth?' cries the heart, as the gull
rocks in changeless estate, and I turn
to my kingdom of sorrowing change.

The Glass Jar

To Vivian Smith

A child one summer's evening soaked
a glass jar in the reeling sun
hoping to keep, when day was done
and all the sun's disciples cloaked
in dream and darkness from his passion fled,
this host, this pulse of light beside his bed.

Wrapped in a scarf his monstrance stood
ready to bless, to exorcise
monsters that whispering would rise
nightly from the intricate wood
that ringed his bed, to light with total power
the holy commonplace of field and flower.

He slept. His sidelong violence summoned
fiends whose mosaic vision saw
his heart entire. Pincer and claw,
trident and vampire fang, envenomed
with his most secret hate, reached and came near
to pierce him in the thicket of his fear.

He woke, recalled his jar of light,
and trembling reached one hand to grope
the mantling scarf away. Then hope
fell headlong from its eagle height.
Through the dark house he ran, sobbing his loss,
to the last clearing that he dared not cross:

the bedroom where his comforter
lay in his rival's fast embrace
and faithless would not turn her face
from the gross violence done to her.
Love's proud executants played from a score
no child could read or realise. Once more

to bed, and to worse dreams he went.
A ring of skeletons compelled
his steps with theirs. His father held
fiddle and bow, and scraped assent
to the malignant ballet. The child dreamed
this dance perpetual, and waking screamed

fresh morning to his window-sill.
As ravening birds began their song
the resurrected sun, whose long
triumph through flower-brushed fields would fill
night's gulfs and hungers, came to wink and laugh
in a glass jar beside a crumpled scarf.

A Postcard

Snow crusts the boughs' austere entanglement.
Bare spines once fleshed in summer's green delights
pattern an ice-green sky. Three huntsmen go
vested for the ritual of the hunt
with lean, anonymous dogs for acolytes.
Shadowless, luminous, their world of snow
superlative in paint: so we assume
on snowlit air mortality's faint plume.

Often in the museum I would stand
before this picture, while my father bent
to teach me its perfections. It became
part of the love that leapt from hand to hand
in a live current; a mind-made continent;
familiar as my shadow or my name
were the near, sprawling arabesque of thorns,
the looping skaters, and the towering horns

the Moses-mountain lifted, gripping its stone
covenant between cold and solitude.
My four-square world! Homesickness, sit in tears
turning the mind's old scrapbook, the long known
pastiche of yesterdays, believing good
and incorruptible the uneasy years
of childhood learning treachery in its slow
budding of cells, and heartsblood on the snow

that day my dolls did not return my kiss.
In their blank eyes all flashing evidence
sank to lack-lustre glass; about me spilled
the shrouding light of a new genesis.
No hand lay palm to mine in innocence.
A blind, beaked hunger, crying to be filled,
nestled and gaped, was fed, and whipped again
in bird-clear syllables of mortal pain

through a rare kingdom crumbling into paint.
A father's magus mantle sleeved no longer
an old man's trembling gestures towards his gift
sealed in with myrrh; and sovereign youth grew faint
hearing that crystal voice cry still the hunger
tented in flesh: 'Time's herod-blade is swift.
Hunt me down love, the snow-white unicorn,
I'll drink in safety from its twisted horn

your childhood's relic poison, and lie quiet.'
Now I am old. The fabulous beast, grown tame,
dreams in heraldic stillness of the chase;
the sick heart, chafed by memory's salt-rough diet,
craves for lost childish sweetness, cannot name
its old heroic themes. My early face
withered to bone, fretted by wintry change,
flowering in blood-bright cheek and lip grows strange:

my children's children, with my father's eyes
stare with me at this postcard, seeing only
a sharp and simple winter, while they wear
the hard sun like a skin. And my love lies
imprisoned in stiff gestures, hearing the lonely
voice call 'I hunger' through the snow-bright air.
Spilling the days no memory will restore
time's fountain climbs its own perpetual core.

'I am the Captain of My Soul'

The human body is the best picture of the human soul.

Ludwig Wittgenstein

But the Captain is drunk, and the crew
hauling hard on his windlass of fury are whipped
by his know–nothing rage. Their terror
troubles the sunlight. 'Now tell me,'
the Captain says, as his drunkenness
drifts into tears, 'what's to keep me
at ease in this harbour?'
                                    'We'll tell you,'
say Hands, 'in our headlong chase through a fugue

for three voices, you heard a fourth voice naming
divisions of silence. We'll summon
that voice once again, it may tell you
of marvels wrung from sorrow endured.'
'We have seen,' say Eyes, 'how in Venice
the steps of churches open and close
like marble fans under water.'

'You can rot in your sockets,' the Captain cries.

'I have children,' says Body, haloed
in tenderness, firm in ripeness still.
'I grew gross with their stress, I went spinning
in a vortex of pain. I gave my breast
and its beauty to nourish their heedless growth.
They jump on my shadow in mischievous joy.
On their lives your astonishing sorrows
flow easy as water on marble steps.'

'Lass sie betteln gehn!' roars the Captain
as his old wounds burn, and he gulps
from his flagon of grief. 'You servants, you things,
stand up there! *You* with the ageing choir-boy face,
and *you* with your facile dexterity, *you*
with your marble hallucinations, COME!'

Hands, eyes, body keel to the void as the drunken
Captain sings in his wilderness of water.

The Waldstein

To Rex Hobcroft

Hands, nerves know this. I mourn for my lost skill,
sitting so close I hear your finger-fall
quick on the keys. Music uncovers all:
in this apocalypse of sound, the will
sees its poor tool, the body, as it is.
Years whiten, spinning in a dance of motes.
Flakes of reality disguised as notes
fall blazing round me.
                Must I come to this
painful self-knowledge now?
                     The world is lit,
warmed, by a molten star. Although I see
by the sun's light I cannot stare at it.
The music speaks with gathering energy,
answers with joy my spirit's questioning.
Burnt clear in this refining fire I sing.

Prize-Giving

Professor Eisenbart, asked to attend
a girls' school speech night as an honoured guest
and give the prizes out, rudely declined;
but from indifference agreed, when pressed
with dry scholastic jokes, to change his mind,
to grace their humble platform, and to lend

distinction (of a kind not specified)
to the occasion. Academic dress
became him, as he knew. When he appeared
the girls whirred with an insect nervousness,
the Head in humbler black flapped round and steered
her guest, superb in silk and fur, with pride

to the best seat beneath half-hearted blooms
tortured to form the school's elaborate crest.
Eisenbart scowled with violent distaste,
then recomposed his features to their best
advantage: deep in thought, with one hand placed
like Rodin's Thinker. So he watched the room's

mosaic of young heads. Blonde, black, mouse-brown
they bent for their Headmistress' opening prayer.
But underneath a light (no accident
of seating, he felt sure), with titian hair
one girl sat grinning at him, her hand bent
under her chin in mockery of his own.

Speeches were made and prizes given. He shook
indifferently a host of virgin hands.
'Music!' The girl with titian hair stood up,
hitched at a stocking, winked at near-by friends,
and stood before him to receive a cup
of silver chased with curious harps. He took

her hand, and felt its voltage fling his hold
from his calm age and power; suffered her strange
eyes, against reason dark, to take his stare
with her to the piano, there to change
her casual schoolgirl's for a master's air.
He forged his rose-hot dream as Mozart told

the fullness of all passion or despair
summoned by arrogant hands. The music ended,
Eisenbart teased his gown while others clapped,
and peered into a trophy which suspended
his image upside down: a sage fool trapped
by music in a copper net of hair.

Boundary Conditions

'At the sun's incredible centre
        the atomic nuclei
with electrons and light quanta
        in a burning concord lie.
All the particles that form
        light and matter, in that furnace
keep their equilibrium.
        Once we pass beyond the surface
of the star, sharp changes come.
        These remarks apply as well
to the exploding atom bomb,'
        said Professor Eisenbart
while his mistress, with a shell
        scored an arrow and a heart
in the sand on which they lay
        watching heat and light depart
from the boundaries of day.

'Sprung from love's mysterious core
        soul and flesh,' the young girl said,
'restless on the narrow shore
        between the unborn and the dead,
split from concord, and inherit
        mankind's old dichotomy:
mind and matter; flesh and spirit;
        what has been and what will be;
desire that flares beyond our fate:
        still in the heart more violence lies
than in the bomb. Who'll calculate
        that tough muscle's bursting size?'

Tongues of darkness licked the crust
        of pigment from the bowl of blue.
Thought's campaniles fell to dust
        blown by the sea-wind through and through.

MAPPINGS OF THE PLANE

Triste, Triste

In the space between love and sleep
when heart mourns in its prison
eyes against shoulder keep
their blood-black curtains tight.
Body rolls back like a stone, and risen
spirit walks to Easter light;

away from its tomb of bone,
away from the guardian tents
of eyesight, walking alone
to unbearable light with angelic
gestures. The fallen instruments
of its passion lie in the relic

darkness of sleep and love.
And heart from its prison cries
to the spirit walking above:
'I was with you in agony.
Remember your promise of paradise,'
and hammers and hammers, 'Remember me.'

So the loved other is held
for mortal comfort, and taken,
and the spirit's light dispelled
as it falls from its dream to the deep
to harrow heart's prison so heart may waken
to peace in the paradise of sleep.

In the Park

She sits in the park. Her clothes are out of date.
Two children whine and bicker, tug her skirt.
A third draws aimless patterns in the dirt.
Someone she loved once passes by – too late

to feign indifference to that casual nod.
'How nice,' *et cetera*. 'Time holds great surprises.'
From his neat head unquestionably rises
a small balloon... 'but for the grace of God...'

They stand awhile in flickering light, rehearsing
the children's names and birthdays. 'It's so sweet
to hear their chatter, watch them grow and thrive,'
she says to his departing smile. Then, nursing
the youngest child, sits staring at her feet.
To the wind she says, 'They have eaten me alive.'

O Could One Write As One Makes Love

O could one write as one makes love
when all is given and nothing kept,
then language might put by at last
its coy elisions and inept
withdrawals, yield, and yielding cast
aside like useless clothes the crust
of worn and shabby use, and trust

its candour to the urgent mind,
its beauty to the searching tongue.
Safe in the world's great house with all
its loves and griefs, at ease among
its earthly fruits, original
as earth and air, the body learns
peace, while the mind in torment burns

to strip the cloak of daily use
from language. Could one seize and move
the stubborn words to yield and sing,
then one would write as one makes love
and poems and revelations spring
like children from the mind's desire,
original as light and fire.

from *Poems/Volume Two*
(1968)

At the Arts Club

Kröte is drunk, but still can play.
Knick-knacks in shadow-boxes wink
at gewgaws while he grinds away
at Brahms, not much the worse for drink.

The hostess pats her tinted curls.
Sees, yawning surreptitiously,
a bitch in black with ginger pearls
squeezing the local tenor's knee.

Kröte lets the loud pedal blur
a dubious trill. The variations
on Handel's foursquare theme occur
to most as odd manipulations

of something better left alone.
They suffer. Kröte knows they do:
with malice adds some more, his own,
and plays all the repeats right through.

He was expected to perform
a waltz, or something short and sweet.
The coffee's made, the supper's warm,
the ravenous guests would love to eat.

Sober, Kröte's inclined to gloom.
Drunk, he becomes a sacred clown.
He puffs and pounds and shakes the room.
An ill-placed ornament falls down.

A pause. Chairs squeak. The hostess claps,
wrongly – there's still the fugue to play.
Tenor and Ginger Pearls, perhaps
for ever, boldly sneak away.

Ebb-tide

Now that you have no word for me
I bring your bitter silence here
where the tide rustles from the land
seaward, its whispered meaning clear.
My young son chases, stone in hand,
a sandcrabs' rattling greyblue army.

He stones the scuttling host, and gathers
one crippled prize. Cannot decide
which is its head. As dying claws
tickle his palm, he laughs. The tide
withdraws for his delight. We pause
at every pool. The mind surrenders

its agony to littoral creatures
rocked in the comfort of the shore's
unvarying seasons. A smooth spine
held in my idle fingers scores
a name in sand as the gulls sign
the windless water with your features.

I have one picture of you taken
picnicking somewhere: mountains, clouds
beyond a pier; incredibly blue
water surrounds you, masts and shrouds
pattern unheard-of azure. You
smile there forever. Time has shaken

life from the sea, flung on dry land
bones that got upright, fleshed their wild
sea-creature grins, and learned the weight
of earth. I run beside my child
stoning the crabs with mindless hate.
The sea withdraws from the gold sand.

Burning Sappho

The clothes are washed, the house is clean.
I find my pen and start to write.
Something like hatred forks between
my child and me. She kicks her good
new well-selected toys with spite
around the room, and whines for food.
Inside my smile a monster grins
and sticks her image through with pins.

The child is fed, and sleeps. The dishes
are washed, the clothes are ironed and aired.
I take my pen. A kind friend wishes
to gossip while she darns her socks.
Scandal and pregnancies are shared.
The child wakes, and the Rector knocks.
Invisible inside their placid
hostess, a fiend pours prussic acid.

Night now. Orion first begins
to show. Day's trivial angers cease.
All is required, until one wins,
at last, this hour. I start to write.
My husband calls me, rich in peace,
to bed. Now deathless verse, good night.
In my warm thighs a fleshless devil
chops him to bits with hell-cold evil.

All's quiet at last: the world, the flesh,
the devils burning in my brain.
Some air of morning stirs afresh
my shaping element. The mind
with images of love and pain
grapples down gulfs of sleep. I'll find
my truth, my poem, and grasp it yet.
    'The moon is gone, the Pleiads set...'

In Brisbane

By the old bridge in flaring sunlight
a ghost is waiting, with my face
of twenty years ago, to show me
the paths I never can retrace.

Here as of old upon the river
float light's beguiling images.
Over a quilt of blue the branches
bend with domestic tenderness.

Here, to my blood's exalted rhythm,
silly with love I'd pace for hours
sifting the piecemeal revelations
of life and time through falling flowers.

Intemperate ghost, who longed to hazard
the pure space of experience,
to bid unheard-of constellations
form from their joyful elements:

these trees that cannot hold their blossom,
the public handsomeness of stone
remain. Your grand abstractions shimmered
like light on water, and are gone.

My ghost, my self, most intimate stranger
standing beneath these lyric trees
with your one wineglassful of morning
snatched from the rushing galaxies,

bright-haired and satin-lipped you offer
the youth I shall not taste again.
I know, I bear to know, your future
unlooked-for love, undreamed-of pain.

With your untempered spirit shatter
the glass of time that keeps apart
what was and is.
                        Through fractured sunlight
I see a less-than-shadow pass

to light again. A cloud of blossom
drifts on the water's changing face
from the blue trees unfolding summer
above my head in sunlit space.

Estuary

To Rex Hobcroft

Wind crosshatches shallow water.
Paddocks rest in the sea's arm.
Swamphens race through spiky grass.
A wire fence leans, a crazy stave
with sticks for barlines, wind for song.
Over us, interweaving light
with air and substance, ride the gulls.

Words in our undemanding speech
hover and blend with things observed.
Syllables flow in the tide's pulse.
My earliest memory turns in air:
eclipse. Cocks crow, as if at sunset;
Grandmother, holding a smoked glass,
says to me, *'Look. Remember this.'*

Over the goldbrown sand my children
run in the wind. The sky's immense
with spring's new radiance. Far from here,
lying close to the final darkness,
a great-grandmother lives and suffers,
still praising life: another morning
on earth, cockcrow and changing light.

Over the skeleton of thought
mind builds a skin of human texture.
The eye's part of another eye
that guides it through the maze of light.
A line becomes a firm horizon.
All's as it was in the beginning.
Obscuring symbols melt away.

'Remember this.' I will remember
this quiet in which the questioning mind
allows reality to enter
its gateway as a friend, unchallenged,
to rest as a friend may, without speaking;
light falling like a benediction
on moments that renew the world.

MAPPINGS OF THE PLANE

Alla Siciliana

To O.B. Dunne

Earthbound, I watch the darting swallows.
In shivering reeds the wind is caught.
Bright water bears away the mind's
unravellings of restless thought.

Sunset's clear-speaking light discloses
in the calm eloquence of stone,
the lapsing syllables of water,
the whispering reeds and grasses blown

to quiet at last, to windfall silence,
another tongue, a language learned
by ear, by heart in earliest childhood,
when earth in its own radiance turned

always from nightmare-dark to morning.
I see that lost enchantment wake
in light, on water, and the spirit
like a loved guest on earth can take

its needs and its delights, and wander
freely. The dazzling moments burn
to time again. In simple twilight
water speaks peace, the swallows turn

in lessening arcs. The dry reeds rustle
and part to set the nightwind free.
The heart holds, like remembered music,
a landscape grown too dark to see.

New Music

To Larry Sitsky

Who can grasp for the first time
these notes hurled into empty space?
Suddenly a tormenting nerve
affronts the fellowship of cells.
Who can tell for the first time
if it is love or pain he feels,
violence or tenderness that calls
plain objects by outrageous names

and strikes new sound from the old names?
At the service of a human vision,
not symbols, but strange presences
defining a transparent void,
these notes beckon the mind to move
out of the smiling context of
what's known; and what can guide it is
neither wisdom nor power, but love.

Who but a fool would enter these
regions of being with no name?
Secure among their towering junk
the wise and powerful congregate
fitting old shapes to old ideas,
rocked by their classical harmonies
in living sleep. The beggars' stumps
bang on the stones. Nothing will change.

Unless, wakeful with questioning,
some mind beats on necessity,
and being unanswered learns to bear
emptiness like a wound that no
word but its own can mend; and finds
a new imperative to summon
a world out of unmeasured darkness
pierced by a brilliant nerve of sound.

MAPPINGS OF THE PLANE

To A.D. Hope

I remember well that evening years ago:
    a woman glittering with rhinestones sighed,
'Professor Hope, how wonderful to know
    a poet in the flesh!' As you replied,

'Well, I am usually present there,'
    a spark of irresponsible delight
flickered between us through the smoky air.
    Over the glossy small-talk of that night

you skimmed and shimmered with a dragonfly
    lightness of conversation, while you stood
solidly present, beaming eye to eye
    at those who filled your glass or brought you food.

Glücklicher Dichter! Poet as smiling man –
    we talked in snatches through the smooth time-killing
talk about art; friendship no older than
    an hour with absolute acceptance filling

old absent hours. The same ridiculous
    thought, that the bardic robes assumed ideally
right might be tattered, had occurred to us:
    hard-working aspirants, perhaps, but really

like Martin Tupper, or Eliza Cook.
    We spoke of early childhood, memories, dreams:
you told me of one dream in which you took
    your place before an orchestra, and themes

sprang instantly from your composing mind
    into the belly of each instrument;
players obedient to no score combined
    while you beat time, composing as you went,

to realise your changing harmonies.
    Dream, parable: the marvellous translation
of thought to act; light that the spirit sees
    flashing through its material creation,

thought shaping with serene authority
      the world of sense – a happy dream, indeed.
Was this perhaps what Adam lost, when he
      and his free-thinking partner felt the need

for some good salty *Angst*, and left the air
      of paradise for ever, with the black
hangdogs of melancholy and despair
      sniffing and snivelling round them on the track

to bodily extinction, word and thing
      no longer one, the running dialogue
of flesh and spirit failing at the spring,
      horizons shrouded in a shifting fog

of doubt – the world, the case, the what-is-given,
      life's opera, death's horror-movie show,
the nagging memory of a long-lost heaven,
      Imperial Adam's gift: all this we know.

But who would call his primal state a blessing?
      Who would not bite the fruit, and bear the change?
How could the heart in an unprepossessing
      coma of innocence have shown its range?

Who in full manhood would remain sincerely
      a child in a child's Eden, and as dumb?
And who on earth would sing, if song were merely
      an effortless warbling until kingdom come?

Poet as hero, nobly present in
      the flesh, now half a continent away;
friend, at whose triumphs won and still to win
      I'll stand rejoicing, though I cannot say

all that I owe, I grapple through the same
      night-watches with self-doubt, suffer the long
torment of waiting for a word to name
      grief that must be resolved in healing song:

accept my praise for the true fables of
        your speaking tongue, for the heart celebrating
its solemn happiness in human love,
        most for the elected spirit recreating

from dream and darkness, through your images,
        the wing-flash of a joy that is no dream:
dragonfly-light, a moment motionless,
        brighter than daylight on the blazing stream.

from *Poems 1969–1974*

Dust to Dust

I dream I stand once more
in Ann Street by the old
fire station. The palms
like feather dusters move
idly in stifling air.
The sky's dusted with gold.
A footfall; someone comes;
I cannot speak for love.

We walk in silence past
All Saints'. The dead do rise,
do live, do walk and wear
their flesh. Your exile's done.
So, so, resume our last
rejoicing kiss. Your eyes
flecked with my image stare
in wonder through my own.

Round us air turns to flame.
Ashes rain from the sky.
A firebell clangs and clangs
insanely as I wake
to absence with your name
shaping my lips. I lie
losing the dream that hangs
fading in air. I shake

the last of night away.
These bright motes that define
morning inside my room
hold not one grain of you.
Another sunstruck day
whose moving dust-motes shine
remote from any dream
cannot restore, renew

our laughter that hot night
when by All Saints' we talked
in the brief time we had.
During *Magnificat*
an urchin stopped to write
on the church wall. He chalked
his message: GOD IS MAD.
I say Amen to that.

An Impromptu for Ann Jennings

Sing, memory, sing those seasons in the freezing
    suburb of Fern Tree, a rock-shaded place
with tree ferns, gullies, snowfalls and eye-pleasing
    prospects from paths along the mountain-face.

Nursing our babies by huge fires of wattle,
    or pushing them in prams when it was fine,
exchanging views on diet, or Aristotle,
    discussing Dr Spock or Wittgenstein,

cleaning up infants and the floors they muddied,
    bandaging, making ends and tempers meet –
sometimes I'd mind your children while you studied,
    or you'd take mine when I felt near defeat;

keeping our balance somehow through the squalling
    disorder, or with anguish running wild
when sickness, a sick joke from some appalling
    orifice of the nightwatch, touched a child;

think of it, woman: each of us gave birth to
    four children, our new lords whose beautiful
tyrannic kingdom might restore the earth to
    that fullness we thought lost beyond recall

when, in the midst of life, we could not name it,
    when spirit cried in darkness, '*I will have…*'
but what? have what? There was no word to frame it,
    though spirit beat at flesh as in a grave

from which it could not rise. But we have risen.
    Caesar's we were, and wild, though we seemed tame.
Now we move where we will. Age is no prison
    to hinder those whose joy has found its name.

We are our own. All Caesar's debts are rendered
    in full to Caesar. Time has given again
a hundredfold those lives that we surrendered,
    the love, the fruitfulness; but not the pain.

Before the last great fires we two went climbing
    like gods or blessed spirits in summer light
with the quiet pulse of mountain water chiming
    as if twenty years were one long dreaming night,

above the leafy dazzle of the streams
    to fractured rock, where water had its birth,
and stood in silence, at the roots of dreams,
    content to know: our children walk the earth.

The Violets

It is dusk, and cold. I kneel to pick
frail melancholy flowers among
ashes and loam. The melting west
is striped like ice-cream. While I try
whistling a trill, close by his nest
        our blackbird frets and strops his beak
indifferent to Scarlatti's song.
Ambiguous light. Ambiguous sky

        Towards nightfall waking from the fearful
        half-sleep of a hot afternoon
        at our first house, in Mitchelton,
        I ran to find my mother, calling
        for breakfast. Laughing, 'It will soon
        be night, you goose,' her long hair falling
        down to her waist, she dried my tearful
        face as I sobbed, 'Where's morning gone?'

        and carried me downstairs to see
        spring violets in their loamy bed.
        Hungry and cross, I would not hold
        their sweetness, or be comforted,
        even when my father, whistling, came
        from work, but used my tears to scold
        the thing I could not grasp or name
        that, while I slept, had stolen from me

        those hours of unreturning light.
        Into my father's house we went,
        young parents and their restless child,
        to light the lamp and the wood stove
        while dusk surrendered pink and white
        to blurring darkness. Reconciled,
        I took my supper and was sent
        to innocent sleep.
                        Years cannot move

nor death's disorienting scale
distort those lamplit presences
      a child with milk and story-book;
      my father, bending to inhale
      the gathered flowers, with tenderness
      stroking my mother's goldbrown hair.
      Stone-curlews call from Kedron Brook.
Faint scent of violets drifts in air.

At Mornington

They told me that when I was taken
to the sea's edge, for the first time,
I leapt from my father's arms
and was caught by a wave and rolled
like a doll among rattling shells;
and I seem to remember my father
fully clothed, still streaming with water
half comforting, half angry.
And indeed I remember believing
as a child, I could walk on water –
the next wave, the next wave –
it was only a matter of balance.

On what flood are they borne,
these memories of early childhood
iridescent, fugitive
as light in a sea-wet shell,
while we stand, two friends of middle age,
by your parents' grave in silence
among avenues of the dead
with their cadences of trees,
marble and granite parting
the quick of autumn grasses.
We have the wholeness of this day
to share as we will between us.

This morning I saw in your garden
fine pumpkins grown on a trellis
so it seemed that the vines were rising
to flourish the fruits of earth
above their humble station
in airy defiance of nature
– a parable of myself,
a skinful of elements climbing
from earth to the fastness of light;
now come to that time of life
when our bones begin to wear us,
to settle our flesh in final shape

as the drying face of land
rose out of earth's seamless waters.
    I dreamed once, long ago,
    that we walked among day-bright flowers
    to a bench in the Brisbane gardens
    with a pitcher of water between us,
    and stayed for a whole day
    talking, and drinking the water.
    Then, as night fell, you said
    'There is still some water left over.'
We have one day, only one,
but more than enough to refresh us.

At your side among the graves
I think of death no more
Than when, secure in my father's arms,
I laughed at a hollowed pumpkin
with candle flame for eyesight,
and when I am seized at last
and rolled in one grinding race
of dreams, pain, memories, love and grief,
from which no hand will save me,
the peace of this day will shine
like light on the face of the waters
that bear me away for ever.

David's Harp

Saturday morning. I rehearse
the Sunday hymns, fortissimo,
in the cool twilight of the church,
adding new stops at every verse.
Someone creaks the west door. I know
I am the object of his search,
gazed at, as though from far away.
He must be thirty, if a day.

I turn my seventeen-year-old
profile a trifle heavenwards,
and hastily reduce the sound,
accommodating to his bold
descant on *David's Harp*. The Lord's
house might as well be Circe's ground.
          'With thee all night I mean to stay,
          and wrestle till the break of day.'

'With thee all night.' So Wesley wrote,
though not with secular intent.
What flourishes that tune will bear!
My tenor wreathes it note by note
in rich Handelian ornament.
Faint burnt-out incense on the air
offends his Presbyterian nose.
He sneezes, stares across the rows

of empty pews between us; still
singing, walks to the organ; stands
beside me; puts his arms around
my waist and squeezes me until
I gasp, then gently lifts my hands
to his, and kisses me. He's sound
of wind. His kiss is long. We share
at last a common need for air.

'Give me one kiss, my bonny lass!'
Vain as a cat, I frown and toss
my head. He watches Brisbane's hot
sunshine, strained through Victorian glass,
lacquer a Station of the Cross.
He scowls and thunders: 'Thou shalt not
make any graven images.'
But as he bends his head to kiss

the image of his hope, the door
moves with its useful warning creak.
He steps aside. I start to play.
He fills his lungs, and sings once more,
       'Speak to me now, in blessings speak.'
A death-pale curate come to pray
kneels, and is forced to find his Lord
through a loud F sharp major chord.

Where's that bright man who loved me, when
there was not much to love? He died
soon after. The undying flow
of music bears him close again,
handsome and young, while I am tried
in time's harsh fires. Dear man, I know
your worth, being now less ignorant of
the nature and the names of love.

Carnal Knowledge   I

Roll back, you fabulous animal
be human, sleep. I'll call you up
from water's dazzle, wheat-blond hills,
clear light and open-hearted roses,
this day's extravagance of blue
stored like a pulsebeat in the skull.

Content to be your love, your fool,
your creature tender and obscene,
I'll bite sleep's innocence away
and wake the flesh my fingers cup
to build a world from what's to hand,
new energies of light and space

wings for blue distance, fins to sweep
the obscure caverns of your heart,
a tongue to lift your sweetness close
leaf-speech against the window-glass
a memory of chaos weeping
mute forces hammering for shape

sea-strip and sky-strip held apart
for earth to form its hills and roses
its landscape from our blind caresses,
blue air, horizon, water-flow,
bone to my bone I grasp the world.
But what you are I do not know.

Carnal Knowledge II

Grasshoppers click and whirr.
Stones grow in the field.
Autumnal warmth is sealed
in a gold skin of light
on darkness plunging down
to earth's black molten core.

Earth has no more to yield.
Her blond grasses are dry.
    Nestling my cheek against
    the hollow of your thigh
    I lay cockeyed with love
    in the most literal sense.

Your eyes, kingfisher blue.
This was the season, this
the light, the halcyon air.
Our window framed this place.
If there were music here,
insectile, abstract, bare,

it would bless no human ear.
Shadows lie with the stones.
Bury our hearts, perhaps
they'll strike it rich in earth's
black marrow, crack, take root,
bring forth vines, blossom, fruit.

    Roses knocked on the glass.
    Wine like a running stream
    no evil spell could cross
    flowed round the house of touch.
God grant me drunkenness
if this is sober knowledge,

song to melt sea and sky
apart, and lift these hills
from the shadow of what was,
and roll them back, and lie
in naked ignorance
in the hollow of your thigh.

Night Thoughts: Baby & Demon

Baby I'm sick. I need
nursing. Give me your breast.
My orifices bleed.
I cannot sleep. My chest
shakes like a window. Light
guts me. My head's not right.

Demon, we're old, old chap.
Born under the same sign
after some classic rape.
Gemini. Yours is mine.
Sickness and health. We'll share
the end of this affair.

Baby, I'm sick to death.
But I can't die. You do
the songs, you've got the breath.
Give them the old soft shoe.
Put on a lovely show.
Put on your wig, and go.

The service station flags, denticulate
plastic, snap in the wind. Hunched seabirds wait

for light to quench the unmeaning lights of town.
This day will bring the fabulous summer down.

Weather no memory can match will fade
to memory, leaf-drift in the pines' thick shade.

All night salt water stroked and shaped the sand.
All night I heard it. Your bravura hand

chimed me to shores beyond time's rocking swell.
The last cars leave the shabby beach motel.

Lovers and drunks unroofed in sobering air
disperse, ghost-coloured in the streetlight-glare.

Rock-a-bye Baby
   in the motel
Baby will kiss
   and Demon will tell.

One candle lights us. Night's cool airs begin
to lick the luminous edges of our skin.

   When the bough bends
      the apple will fall
   Baby knows nothing
      Demon knows all.

Draw up the voluptuously crumpled sheet.
In rose-dark silence gentle tongues repeat
the body's triumph through its grand eclipse.
I feel your pulsebeat through my fingertips.

   Baby's a rocker
      lost on the shore.
   Demon's a mocker.
      Baby's a whore.

World of the happy, innocent and whole:
the body's the best picture of the soul
couched like an animal in savage grace.
Ghost after ghost obscures your sleeping face.

   My baby's like a bird of day
      that flutters from my side,
   my baby's like an empty beach
      that's ravished by the tide.

   So fair are you, my bonny lass,
      so sick and strange am I,
   that I must lie with all your loves
      and suck your sweetness dry.

   And drink your juices dry, my dear,
      and grind your bones to sand,
   then I will walk the empty shore
      and sift you through my hand.

And sift you through my hand, my dear,
   and find you grain by grain,
and build your body bone by bone
   and flesh those bones again,

with flesh from all your loves, my love,
   while tides and seasons stream,
until you wake by candle-light
   from your midsummer dream,

and like some gentle creature meet
   the huntsman's murderous eye,
and know you never shall escape
   however fast you fly.

Unhoused I'll shout my drunken songs
   and through the streets I'll go
compelling all I meet to toast
   the bride they do not know.

Till all your tears are dry, my love,
   and your ghosts fade in the sun.
Be sure I'll have your heart, my love,
   when all your loving's done.

Meditation on Wyatt   II

'Forget not yet, forget not this'
       We are what darkness has become:
       two bodies bathed in saffron light
       disarmed by sudden distances
       pitched on the singing heights of time
       our skin aflame with eastern airs,
       changed beyond reason, but not rhyme.

'The which so long hath thee so loved'
       counting the pulsebeats   foot to foot
       our splendid metres   limb to limb
       sweet assonance of tongue and tongue
       figures of speech to speech   bemused
       with metaphors as unimproved
       as the crooked roads of genius

       but our hearts' rhymes are absolute.

'Thought Is Surrounded by a Halo'

Ludwig Wittgenstein, *Philosophical Investigations 97*

Show me the order of the world,
the hard-edge light of this-is-so
prior to all experience
and common to both world and thought,
no model, but the truth itself.

    Language is not a perfect game,
    and if it were, how could we play?
    The world's more than the sum of things
    like moon, sky, centre, body, bed,
    as all the singing masters know.

    Picture two lovers side by side
    who sleep and dream and wake to hold
    the real and the imagined world
    body by body, word by word
    in the wild halo of their thought.

Father and Child

I *Barn Owl*

Daybreak: the household slept.
I rose, blessed by the sun.
A horny fiend, I crept
out with my father's gun.
Let him dream of a child
obedient, angel-mild –

old No-Sayer, robbed of power
by sleep. I knew my prize
who swooped home at this hour
with daylight-riddled eyes
to his place on a high beam
in our old stables, to dream

light's useless time away.
I stood, holding my breath,
in urine-scented hay,
master of life and death,
a wisp-haired judge whose law
would punish beak and claw.

My first shot struck. He swayed,
ruined, beating his only
wing, as I watched, afraid
by the fallen gun, a lonely
child who believed death clean
and final, not this obscene

bundle of stuff that dropped,
and dribbled through loose straw
tangling in bowels, and hopped
blindly closer. I saw
those eyes that did not see
mirror my cruelty

while the wrecked thing that could
not bear the light nor hide
hobbled in its own blood.
My father reached my side,
gave me the fallen gun.
'End what you have begun.'

I fired. The blank eyes shone
once into mine, and slept.
I leaned my head upon
my father's arm, and wept,
owl-blind in early sun
for what I had begun.

II *Nightfall*

Forty years, lived or dreamed:
what memories pack them home.
Now the season that seemed
incredible is come.
Father and child, we stand
in time's long-promised land.

Since there's no more to taste
ripeness is plainly all.
Father, we pick our last
fruits of the temporal.
Eighty years old, you take
this late walk for my sake.

Who can be what you were?
Link your dry hand in mine,
my stick-thin comforter.
Far distant suburbs shine
with great simplicities.
Birds crowd in flowering trees,

sunset exalts its known
symbols of transience.
Your passionate face is grown
to ancient innocence.
Let us walk for this hour
as if death had no power

or were no more than sleep.
Things truly named can never
vanish from earth. You keep
a child's delight for ever
in birds, flowers, shivery-grass –
I name them as we pass.

'Be your tears wet?' You speak
as if air touched a string
near breaking-point. Your cheek
brushes on mine. Old king,
your marvellous journey's done.
Your night and day are one

as you find with your white stick
the path on which you turn
home with the child once quick
to mischief, grown to learn
what sorrows, in the end,
no words, no tears can mend.

from *The Lion's Bride*
(1981)

The Lion's Bride

I loved her softness, her warm human smell,
her dark mane flowing loose. Sometimes stirred by
rank longing laid my muzzle on her thigh.
Her father, faithful keeper, fed me well,
but she came daily with our special bowl
barefoot into my cage, and set it down:
our love feast. We became the talk of town,
brute king and tender woman, soul to soul.

Until today: an icy spectre sheathed
in silk minced to my side on pointed feet.
I ripped the scented veil from its unreal
head and engorged the painted lips that breathed
our secret names. A ghost has bones, and meat!
Come soon my love, my bride, and share this meal.

Mappings of the Plane

All those scales we rehearsed
on other instruments
useless. Our fingering
opened such intervals
and crazy fugues we were
live drunk with space. We scaled

each other. On our skins
the bloom of moisture. Given
the centre of reflection
we are glassed, an ordered pair.
Given our mad notation
we'll find a tune no air

can ruffle. Recombine
our elements. We are
real numbers, and perhaps
the solution is unique.
Reduced to the absurd
wrap ourselves in dry sheets.

I am cooled to this transparency. Recharge me.
Water, I give you leave to enter me,
cold water blazing with a light of harvests.

'It was a summer's day at harvest-time' –
stories begin so. Cloudlight shone like glass
in mild midwinter. All the leaves were still.

Now let all those who drank with us remember
how I was hung with earrings from the plane
trees' numberless resource, 'and thou beside me.'

Let those ill-tempered blades sent out to assault us
slice through the inverse mappings of the plane
at shadows. We preserve our distances.

I am high on acid rock, on wandering glitter.
Sunset lights the King's sails with mocking splendour.
South and south the white sea-eagle hunts

as if he feared his quarry gone for ever.
His wingbeat gleams and vanishes in light.
I am hungry, tearing oysters from the rocks

My hands bleed, and I bathe them in the water
which takes my blood to heart, and changes colour.
Hölderlin, Nerval, Lenz, Novalis, Trakl,

night's actors gather close in darkening wings,
and reach for me: Isolde on the rocks.
But I am poured out for a drier throat.

We shall walk again by water under plane-trees.
Sweet weather will recharge our cup of laughter,
the clattering weathercocks revolve with song.

Something more than wind moves in the leaves,
a new interpretation of their shade
where trees lace arms together. Something grieves:
autumnal breath whose perfect intonation
calls out of nothing all the sobbing airs.
Such ripeness, steady: golden ash still firm,
poplars abiding in their spires of light;
and sadness welling from the shades below.

Leaves conjured off, you wait in sombre
trunks, my desolate harlequins.
Wind shakes your earrings without number.
A council gardener begins
to prune your wands. Black prophet crow
flaps from the rustling drifts below
to his old testament of air
to pick himself a newborn eye.
The clouds mass close like poodle hair,
or lamb fleece, in a frozen sky.
The heart's a carnival, the mind
a cloudy mirror gone half blind.

Let me be your golden child.
Father Aether, lift me high,
let the darkening gold of churches
shade the souls for whom Christ died.
When the cataclysmic waters
wash towards chaos, let me be
your golden child aloft on discourse,
tell me what I long to hear:
that the tiger's bones shall mend,
and the mammoth finish eating
all his sweet Siberian grasses.
Let the arctic corals flourish,
let me be your golden child.
Take me past the bounds of silence.
Let me cross your ordered fields
rolling in the flowers of nonsense,
let me understand my dreams
through the language as it is.
Since the world and life are one,
let me be your golden child.

Evening, Oyster Cove

What is history to me? Mine is the first and only world.

Wittgenstein

The early painters had it right:
    closefisted gums, hills humped on hills,
chill distances where the heart might
    stop in its tracks for loneliness.

Calm tide. My solitary wake
    arrows the glistening waterskin.
Crows, bound for Bruny. Wingbeats make
    the sound of runners breathing, in

their firm compacted paths of air.
    Sunset pours golden syrup on
the northern sandstone. Treetops flare
    briefly, and then the sun is gone.

My geese call from the western rise –
    Babydoll, Fido, Stagolee –
the haunting wildness of their cries
    mocks well-fed domesticity.

This elbow of the shallow bay
    crooked an unchilded dying race
whose liquid language ebbed away.
    Shadows forgather in this place:

Jackey, Patty, Queen Caroline,
    Lalla Rookh – white contemptuous names
cloaked the heartsickness of decline.
    The Governor brought them children's games,

toys, marbles, balls. Let history write
    death after hopeless death. The sea's
a sheet of melancholy light.
    Herons half made of shadow seize

their meal, like necromancers search
   obscuring crystal for a sign.
My boat grounds gently on the beach.
   Home to books, fire and chilled white wine.

Ghosts of the night mist, set me free.
   Forgive, until the past is called
wisdom, and history can be
   told in some last redeeming world.

Wittgenstein and Engelmann

Olmutz, Moravia: Wittgenstein
   is walking side by side
with Engelmann, who lived to write
   after his friend had died,

'I sought, between the world that is
   and the world that ought to be,
in my own troubled self the source
   of the discrepancy,

'and in his lonely mind this touched
   a sympathetic chord.
I offered friendship, and was given
   his friendship, a reward

'no gift of mine could match.' They walk
   as friends do, late at night,
two men of cultivated taste
   talking, in reason's light,

of music (Wittgenstein had learned
   to play the clarinet;
could whistle, too, in perfect pitch,
   one part from a quartet)

and of the pure veracity
   Wittgenstein prized in art.
'Count Eberhard's Hawthorn', Uhland's poem,
   profoundly touched his heart:

Felicitous, simple: Eberhard
   rode by a hawthorn spray,
and in his iron helmet placed
   a tender sprig of may,

which, preserved through the wars, he brought
    home from his pilgrimage.
It grew into a branching tree
    to shelter his old age.

Above his dreams a flowering arch
    by whispering breezes fanned
recalled the far time when he was
    young, in the Holy Land.

One day when Wittgenstein was ill
    and could not leave his bed,
Engelmann's mother sent her son
    with gruel to see him fed.

Engelmann climbing up the stairs
    slipped with the saucepan full,
and steaming oatmeal porridge splashed
    his coat of threadbare wool.

'You are showering me with kindnesses,'
    said grateful Wittgenstein,
and Engelmann, 'I am showering,
    it seems, this coat of mine.'

– *He was mightily amused.* The stiff
    unfunny joke survives
through solemn reminiscences
    to illuminate two lives.

Philosopher and architect
    walk through the flaking town,
Wittgenstein in his uniform
    of red and chocolate brown,

formal and courteous they talk
    of the Count's hawthorn flower;
how nature and our thought conform
    through words' mysterious power;

how propositions cannot state
    what they make manifest;
of the ethical and mystical
    that cannot be expressed;

how the world is on one side of us,
    and on the other hand
language, the mirror of the world;
    and God is, *how things stand.*

Europe lies sick in its foul war.
    Armies choke in clay.
But these friends keep their discourse clear
    as the white hawthorn spray,

one a great genius, and both
    humble enough to seek
the simple sources of that truth
    whereof one cannot speak.

A Quartet for Dorothy Hewett

I *Twilight*

Twilight. Field-mouse light. They rustle
in shadowy palaces of hay.
My old cat, Mr Gabriel Fur,
would hunt to keep the mice away
and like a Harlem Globetrotter
juggle his prizes in the air.

Let the mice fear the owl's soft rush
now their lithe enemy is gone
to nourish a viburnum bush.
On his last night on earth he came
to grizzle gently at my door,
then lay beside me, fur to skin.

Did he recall who killed Cock Robin
when we rose up to earliest birdsong?
'We do not live to experience death,'
said my favourite philosopher
(thinking perhaps about his own).
Tell me what I experience, then,

when I wake to open the house door
hearing a cry I cannot hear,
or when I walk in the scythed field
watching the world give up its light,
and feel ghost-footed at my back
a presence in the rustling stack.

II *Goose-girl*

Darkness my refuge, sleep my consolation
hold me a moment on the crest of sunrise.
Out of the false lucidity of dreams I
           know myself waking.

Now I will walk as if you were beside me
hearing the birds' ancestral incantations.
Light turns familiar landscape to a spectral
        anguish of strangeness.

We were like princes choosing their disguises,
meeting at last in joyful recognition,
laughing unmasked at life, the royal game, whose
        rules are all fatal.

Mantled in snow my white, my grey geese nested.
Now they walk safely with their golden children
knowing the hand that feeds them is immortal:
        I am their goddess.

Where are you now, who came through dream and darkness
bodied in light, whom light dissolves to absence?
How will you know me, barefoot in the pasture,
        dressed as a goose-girl?

Under the poem of words there shines another,
like a gold flagon arrogantly buried
by one who knows that earth itself will yield it
        to the true lover.

III *A Simple Story*

A visiting conductor
        when I was seventeen,
took me back to his hotel room
        to cover the music scene.

I'd written a composition.
        Would wonders never cease –
here was a real musician
        prepared to hold my piece.

He spread my score on the counterpane
        with classic casualness,
and put one hand on the manuscript
        and the other down my dress.

It was hot as hell in The Windsor.
        I said I'd like a drink.
We talked across gin and grapefruit,
        and I heard the ice go clink

as I gazed at the lofty forehead
        of one who led the band,
and guessed at the hoarded sorrows
        no wife could understand.

I dreamed of a soaring passion
        as an egg might dream of flight,
while he read my crude sonata.
        If he'd said, 'That bar's not right,'

or, 'Have you thought of a coda?'
        or, 'Watch that first repeat,'
or, 'Modulate to the dominant,'
        he'd have had me at his feet.

But he shuffled it all together,
        and said, 'That's *lovely*, dear,'
as he put it down on the washstand
        in a way that made it clear

that I was no composer.
        And I being young and vain,
removed my lovely body
        from one who'd scorned my brain.

I swept off like Miss Virtue
        down dusty Roma Street,
and heard the goods trains whistle
        WHO? WHOOOOOO? in aching heat.

MAPPINGS OF THE PLANE

IV *Dorothy, Reading in Hobart*

Lustrous angel, who, if I cried, would hear me,
I call you woman, goddess, muse.
In your dress like the blue between clouds
come out of Tartarus singing
the worst of truth in your voice of shadow.

Truth is humbling. Truth is the last tram
you have to catch, and strap-hang, or not get home.
Truth is the watchman running to King David
with news to weep at, words to tighten harpstrings
like plucked hair. Truth's a court for owls,
a motel room where nymphs and satyrs
howl for Nembutal, reclining
in odd conjunction, now-and-never
coupling their life sentences.
Truth will dash out our teeth.

Sing the love-letters never posted,
the lovely game where art is wasted.
Voice of lustre, voice of shadow,
sing the brightness turned to sadness,
death of the suburbs, death of habit,
spirits bowed in milky sweetness,
sing Tennysonian afternoons
when history sighed and harvests parted
over most unhappy shades.

A woman still as a Dutch painting
takes her pen, the old-gold light
cracks itself to mirror-splinters.

Charm with your haunting vox humana
Merlin from his malign enchantment.
Melt the black frost, mysterious angel.
Heaven's long emptied of its gods.
Fill the void with a woman's voice.

'Let Sappho Have the Singing Head'

Dorothy Hewett, *The Inheritors*

I *Evensong*

A grotesque moon, waxing close,
it hovers late in twilight
raven dark, parrot green.
I say, who let you in?
I was listening to Caruso.
You smell of earth, I don't
want bloody conversation.

I turn the music off.
The Head declares itself:
   'Horrors and deeds of horror
   death from the world's beginning
   dreams known to all the living
   peaceful and wrathful gods
   drift of unhappy ghosts

   I change, singing whatever
   cannot be solved or changed.'
I think of Mahler shouting
at his orchestra, TOO LOUD!
before a note was played.
Cool it, cool it, I say.
Sing this ordinary day.

II *The Head Sings, to a Guitar*

Crazy baby, don't think I'm a doll
   you can kiss and throw down on the mat
like a child who knows nothing at all
   of loving and where it's at.

Don't think you can turn me over
     and hope I will sing *ma-ma*.
You've made a mistake, old lover.
     I'll tell you how things are

in words that will really astound you
     and scratch your self-esteem
while the suburbs twinkle around you
     and the ribs of water gleam

and nursemaid conscience assures you
     that bogies lurk in the yard
and crackling with virtue pours you
     the milk of self-regard.

In darkness I'll find your door
     and softly, softly come through
and bite your veins and pour
     my nightmares into you

and lie at your side unmoving
     while you scream and scream in the night.
It will be too late for loving
     when nurse comes with the light.

III *Diotima*

I am curved, a shadow in crystal
and cannot break through to the world,
so reach for my one drug, music,
and turn it on. It's Caruso.
He is singing *M'appari*.

Well, let life imitate art.
A tenor sings, 'Like a dream',
and a woman sits still and listens.
I feel the drug take hold
of my body, a lover's touch,

as I stare bemused at the fire
and hear the soft rustle of coals
orange hot from the heart of some tree
in a dialogue of passion
darkening, descending to charcoal.

And the scratched old record glows
with the fire of that marvellous voice
too dear for death's possessing.
For pain to exist in the world
there must be a creature to feel it.

Return: I will change you heads.
Have mine, it has no illusions
about being tried in the balance
of God and the suburbs and found
wanting. Take up this coal

still glowing, to set on your tongue.
Sing me the local swans
flying low over luminous water
and the usual crows in the west
croaking, to have the taste

in your mouth and know the wine gone:
that is the anguish of thirst.
Sing me the spectrum of pain
as I sit with your head for mine
steady and cool, not reaching

for the holy saving poison:
to dream my death. The half moon
like a slice of fruit newly cut
moves westward in frosty air.
My tongue has known you. The world

turns on to the shadow of night.
I watch the sparks fly upward,
the fire consuming itself.
There is music of former times
at our place of parting. I wait

as the soul might wait in the grave
through the body's decomposition
from dream to dream of a summer's day
with the half moon swinging westward
desire bleeding away.

A Valediction

As always after partings, I
get from its place the Oxford Donne,
inked in with aches from adolescence.

Who needs drugs if she has enough
uppers and downers in her head?
Though names are not engraved herein,

who can be literally dead
if he leaps from an underlining
into my flesh at *The Sunne Rising*?

Lou Salomé in her old age: 'Whether
I kissed Nietzsche on Monte Sacro
I find I do not now remember.'

Young Saint Thérèse of Lisieux, writing
'When I love, it is forever.'
One mistress of half Europe, one

enclosed with a transcendent lover.
Dear ladies, shall we meet halfway
between sanctity and liberation?

Today I leave the book unopened.
Strangely, this farewell's left me joyful.
Can ghosts die? Yes, old ghosts are summoned

back to their shades of ink. My lover
will come again to me, my body
to its true end will give him joy.

Now in his absence let me walk
at peaceful sunset in the pasture
feeding my geese, my latter children,

and when the afterglow is gone
Lou's ravishing forgetfulness
will rock my soul with saving laughter,

and the singlehearted saint will braid
all loves into one everlasting.
Then, if I need a lullaby,

good Doctor Donne, will you attend?

A Little Night Music

Listen, I will remind you
of what you have never known.
That's what our dreams are for,
and I will be your dream,
a ravishing latecomer
under your handsome skin.
Late, late this night I'll find you

where nothing has a name,
where any page you turn
will long have lost its meaning.
Remember me, while music
melts you to understanding.
Sleep, while new planets burn,
and I will be your dream.

Frost ghosts autumnal pastures.
Though my step is light, my geese
sound their alarm, the plover
scream at me, an intruder
in sleepless fields, and over
your absence measureless
silence extends the stars.

The Sea Anemones

Grey mountains, sea and sky. Even the misty
seawind is grey. I walk on lichened rock
in a kind of late assessment, call it peace.
Then the anemones, scarlet, gouts of blood.
There is a word I need, and earth was speaking.
I cannot hear. These seaflowers are too bright.
Kneeling on rock, I touch them through cold water.
My fingers meet some hungering gentleness.
A newborn child's lips moved so at my breast.
I woke, once, with my palm across your mouth.
> The word is: *ever*. Why add salt to salt?
> Blood drop by drop among the rocks they shine.
> *Anemos*, wind. The spirit, where it will.
Not flowers, no, animals that must eat or die.

Death Has No Features of His Own

Death has no features of his own.
He'll take a young eye bathed in brightness
and the raging cheekbones of a raddled queen.
Misery's cured by his appalling taste.
His house is without issue. He appears
garlanded with lovebirds, hearts and flowers.
Anything, everything.
                                    He'll wear my face and yours.
Not as we were, thank God. As we shall be
when we let go of the world, late ripe fruit falling.
What we are is beyond him utterly.

A Scattering of Ashes

Music alone can make me hold
my breath, thinks Kröte as he catches
his bus. A chill wind sighs. Bone cold
he rubs his hands as something scratches
a blank part of his memory.
Today's not right. Where should he be?

      Beethoven's funeral. Torchbearer
      Schubert held lilies bound in black;
      afterwards with Randhartinger
      and Lachner, heavy of heart, went back
      to the Mahlgrüber Inn, to toast
      the one whom death would summon first.

      Schubert himself.
                     Kröte recalls
      why death is showing him its sting,
      and why he thinks of funerals:
      he must attend a Scattering
      of Ashes, is engaged to play
      at the crematorium today.

There he arrives immersed in gloom.
An earlier customer's not through.
The mourners, in a waiting room,
wait, since there's nothing else to do.
An old lady leans close to say,
'My beloved friend knew Massenet.'

Kröte's impressed. 'And Saint-Saëns too.
She was in Fauré's singing class.
Now I don't know what I shall do.
I thought I'd be the first to pass
away. We were friends for fifty years.'
She weeps, and Kröte's close to tears.

They are summoned. Kröte lifts the lid
of a fancy electronic job.
Is this an organ? God forbid.
He fiddles off a plastic knob,
fumbles the pedals with cold feet,
plays what's required, and takes a seat

beside Old Friend while prayers are said.
The chapel's neutral, shiny-clean.
No reason here to bow the head.
What God would visit this cool scene?
– O for a gorgeous requiem.
Old mittened claws: he watches them

extract from her capacious purse
a small carved wooden box, maybe
a reliquary made to nurse
an ash or two? She taps his knee
and puts the casket, like a grand
actress, in his unwilling hand.

– Pins? Needles? 'Whiskers! Our dead cats.
We've made provision in our wills
for those outliving us.' She pats
his hand confidingly. He spills
the box and contents on the floor.
Mourners are filing through a door,

but Kröte's kneeling to retrieve
whiskers. The cat is on the mat.
Lord, help me find them. I'll believe
in the resurrection of the cat.
She whispers on without concern,
'We couldn't keep whole cats to burn.

'Yes, fifty years we lived together.
Cats were our children.' Kröte leads
her gently into funeral weather
just as an unseen agent feeds
the ashes from a cross-shaped vent.
She shakes her casket. Whiskers sent

flying off on a sudden gust
fall on the unsuspecting crowd.
– Whiskers to whiskers, dust to dust.
'The Cat's Fugue!' she exclaims aloud.
Kröte begins to hum the theme
and feels her crazy joke redeem

the dismal day. He takes her arm.
She smiles at him, and he can guess
how bright she was, how full of charm.
– Such intervals! Let music bless
all hopes, all loves, however odd.
Music, my joy, my full-scale God.

Dialogue

If an angel came with one wish
I might say, deliver that child
who died before birth, into life.
Let me see what she might have become.
He would bring her into a room
fair skinned   the bones of her hands
would press on my shoulderblades
in our long embrace

                  we would sit
with the albums spread on our knees:
now here are your brothers   and here
your sister here the old house
among trees and espaliered almonds.
  – But where am I?
                  Ah my dear
I have only one picture
                 here
in my head   I saw you lying
still folded   one moment   forever
your head bent down to your heart
eyes closed on unspeakable wisdom
your delicate frog-pale fingers

                  spread
apart as if you were playing
a woodwind instrument.
       – My name?
               It was never given.
       – Where is my grave?
              In my head   I suppose
the hospital burnt you.
       – Was I beautiful?
           To me.
       – Do you mourn for me every day?
Not at all   it is more than thirty years
I am feeling the coolness of age
the perspectives of memory change.
Pearlskull   what lifts you here
from night-drift to solemn ripeness?

Mushroom dome? Gourd plumpness?
The frog in my pot of basil?

      – It is none of these, but a rhythm
      the bones of my fingers   dactylic
      rhetoric smashed from your memory.
      Forget me again.
                      Had I lived
      no rhythm would be the same
      nor my brothers and sister feast
      in the world's eternal house.

Overhead   wings of cloud
     burning   and under my feet
          stones marked with demons' teeth.

Mother Who Gave Me Life

Mother who gave me life
I think of women bearing
women. Forgive me the wisdom
I would not learn from you.

It is not for my children I walk
on earth in the light of the living.
It is for you, for the wild
daughters becoming women,

anguish of seasons burning
backward in time to those other
bodies, your mother, and hers
and beyond, speech growing stranger

on thresholds of ice, rock, fire,
bones changing, heads inclining
to monkey bosom, lemur breast,
guileless milk of the word.

I prayed you would live to see
Halley's Comet a second time.
The Sister said, When she died
she was folding a little towel.

You left the world so, having lived
nearly thirty thousand days:
a fabric of marvels folded
down to a little space.

At our last meeting I closed
the ward door of heavy glass
between us, and saw your face
crumple, fine threadbare linen

worn, still good to the last,
then, somehow, smooth to a smile
so I should not see your tears.
Anguish: remembered hours:

a lamp on embroidered linen,
my supper set out, your voice
calling me in as darkness
falls on my father's house.

from *Bone Scan*
(1988)

Class of 1927

Slate

Quite often in some trendy quarter
the passion to redecorate
those areas concerned with water
results in an expanse of slate.
Cork tiling's warmer, vinyl's neater.
Slate's forty dollars a square metre.
In kitchen, laundry, loo, I see
the stuff the State School gave us free,
and very soon my morbid, chronic
nostalgia swells to recreate
slate-pencil's piercing squeal on slate,
beloved of all those bored demonic
infants whose purpose was to make
mischief purely for mischief's sake.

We sat, ranked by examination,
those with the best marks at the back.
In undisguised discrimination
at the front sat the dim, the slack,
where they could not converse or fiddle;
and in the undistinguished middle
the hard triers, the fairly bright
laboured to get their set work right
not out of any love of study
but simply to escape the cane.
Somehow the teacher knew whose brain
was cleared by stirring, whose was muddy.
One vacant lad, condemned to go
from year to year in the front row,

was said to have three skulls, poor creature.
Everyone liked to feel his head
and demonstrate its curious feature:
ridge after ridge of bone instead
of brain. Bonehead was oddly charming.
His eagerness was so disarming
the whole class used him as a pet

though he was likely to forget
between instruction and retrieval
the object he was sent to find.
No angst stirred his unleavened mind.
He beamed, and hummed, and knew no evil.
The doctor's son, a clever skite,
found inexpressible delight

in cruelty. This boy collected,
or stole, unpleasant instruments;
with these, at playtime, he dissected
lizards and frogs, or spiked their vents
to see how long they took in dying.
One day the class, kept in for sighing
when Sir set homework, heard a squeak.
Being on our honour not to speak
while Sir was briefly absent (bearing
his cane as always) we turned round
and witnessed, as the source of sound,
a captive mouse, its torturer swearing
because the victim tried to bite.
The back row, silent out of fright,

did nothing, and the middle section
saw, but pretended not to look.
Bonehead, after a brief inspection,
stopped smiling; turned again and took
his slate out of its slot; descended
in fury, and with one blow ended
the wanton vivisector's sport.
Then revolution of a sort
broke out. The stricken head was gory.
We stamped and cheered our hero on.
The unhappy mouse was too far gone
to benefit from Bonehead's glory,
or squeak for victory, or curse
the arrangement of this universe.

When Sir returned the class was sitting
so quietly he racked his wits
and stroked his cane and walked round hitting
his leg, but didn't find the bits

of slate we hid in hasty cleaning.
Nor did he grasp the hidden meaning
of some congealing drops of red.
'Where did you get that bloody head?'
'Knocked it.' 'Go home. That cut needs dressing.'
Our golden silence filled the room.
We sat preparing to resume
our work as if it were a blessing
to write on slate, for Sir to see,
the conjugation of *to be*.

The Spelling Prize

Every Child's Book of Animal Stories.
To compete, we stood on the wooden forms
that seated four in discomfort.
When you missed your word, you sat down
and wrote it out twenty times.
At last only two were left:
Ella and I, who had sailed
past *ghost*, *nymph*, *scheme*, *flight*, *nephew*,
the shoals of o - u - g - h
and i before e, stood waiting
for the final word. Whoever
put her hand up first when Sir
announced it, could try to spell it.
A pause, while Sir went outside.
Some of the girls started hissing,
'Give Ella a chance. Let her win.'

Through the window I saw the playground
bare as a fowlyard, the ditch
in a paddock beyond where frogs
lived out whatever their life was
before the big boys impaled them
on wooden skewers, a glint
from a roof in the middle distance
that was Ella's home. I had been there
the week before, when my grandmother went
to take their baby, the ninth,
my brother's old shawl. Ella coaxed me

to a ramshackle tinroofed shed
where her father was killing a bull calf.
A velvety fan of blood
opened out on the concrete floor
as one of her brothers pumped the forelegs:
'You do this to empty the heart.'

The father severed the head, and set it
aside on a bench where the eyes, still trusting,
looked back at what had become
of the world. It was not the sight
of the entrails, the deepening crimson
of blood that sent me crying
across the yard, but the calf's eyes watching
knife, whetstone, carcase, the hand that fed.

Ella followed. 'I'll show you my toys.'
In that house where nobody owned
a corner, a space they might call their own,
she kept two old dolls in a shoebox.
Below me the whispers continued:
'Let Ella win the prize.'
Why, now, does memory brood
on Sir's return, and the moment

when he put down his cane and smoothed
his hair grease-tight on his skull
and snapped out the last word: MYSTIC,
a word never found in our Readers.
My innocent hand flew up.
Sheer reflex, but still, I knew it,
and knew I could slip in a k
or an i for a y and lose,

but did not, and sixty years
can't change it; I stand in the playground
and the pale dust stirs as my friends
of the hour before yell 'Skite!'
and 'Showoff!' and 'Think you're clever!'
They gather round Ella, who turns
one hurt look from her red-rimmed eyes
at my coveted, worthless prize.

Religious Instruction

The clergy came in once a week for Religious Instruction.
Divided by faith, not age, we were bidden to be,
(except for the Micks and a Jew) by some curious deduction
Presbyterian, Methodist, Baptist or C of E.

The Micks were allowed to be useful, to tidy the playground.
But Micah, invited to join them, told Sir 'They'd only
give me a hiding', and stayed inside; moved round
as he chose with his book of Hebrew letters, a lonely

example, among the tender lambs of Jesus,
of good behaviour. Handsome as a dark angel
he studied while the big boys laboured to tease us
with hair-tweak, nib-prick, Chinese burns, as the well

of boredom overflowed in games of noughts
and crosses, spitballs, and drawings so obscene
if Sir had found them they'd have earned us six cuts.
'You give me real insight into original sin,'

said one minister in despair, intercepting some verses
describing him as Old Swivelneck. Beaked like a sparrowhawk
he clawed at his collar and singled me out from his class.
I feared his anger rightly, feared he would talk

to our headmaster, or Sir. I stood in disgrace.
Then a quiet voice from the back interrupted his wrath:
'I am ready to forgive.' 'Who said that? Stand up in your place!'
Micah stood. 'It was said by the Lord God of Sabaoth.'

Then we heard the monitor's footsteps. Saved by the bell!
In a tumult of voices we spilled into sunlight to play,
a host of rejoicing sinners, too young to feel
original darkness under that burning day.

The Twins

Three years old when their mother died
in what my grandmother called
accouchement, my father labour,
they heard the neighbours intone
'A mercy the child went with her.'

Their father raised them somehow.
No one could tell them apart.
At seven they sat in school
in their rightful place, at the top
of the class, the first to respond
with raised arm and finger-flick.

When one gave the answer, her sister
repeated it under her breath.
An inspector accused them of cheating,
but later, in front of the class,
declared himself sorry, and taught us
a marvellous word: *telepathic*.

On Fridays, the story went,
they slept in the shed, barred in
from their father's rage as he drank
his dead wife back to his house.
For the rest of the week he was sober
and proud. My grandmother gave them
a basket of fruit. He returned it.
'We manage. We don't need help.'

They could wash their own hair, skin rabbits,
milk the cow, make porridge, clean boots.

Unlike most of the class I had shoes,
clean handkerchiefs, ribbons, a toothbrush.
We all shared the schoolsores and nits
and the language I learned to forget
at the gate of my welcoming home.

One day as I sat on the fence
my pinafore goffered, my hair
still crisp from the curlers, the twins
came by. I scuttled away
so I should not have to share

my Saturday sweets. My mother
saw me, and slapped me, and offered
the bag to the twins, who replied
one aloud and one *sotto voce*,
'No thank you. We don't like lollies.'

They lied in their greenish teeth
as they knew, and we knew.
                              Good angel
give me that morning again
and let me share, and spare me
the shame of my parents' rebuke.

If there are multiple worlds
then let there be one with an ending
quite other than theirs: leaving school
too early and coming to grief.

Or if this is our one life sentence,
hold them in innocence, writing
Our Father which art in Heaven
in copperplate, or drawing
(their work being done) the same picture
on the backs of their slates: a foursquare
house where a smiling woman
winged like an angel welcomes
two children home from school.

Bone Scan

Thou hast searched me and known me. Thou knowest my downsitting and mine uprising.

Psalm 139

In the twinkling of an eye,
in a moment, all is changed:
on a small radiant screen
(honeydew melon green)
are my scintillating bones.
Still in my flesh I see
the God who goes with me
glowing with radioactive
isotopes. This is what he
at last allows a mortal
eye to behold: the grand
supporting frame complete
(but for the wisdom teeth),
the friend who lives beneath
appearances, alive
with light. Each glittering bone
assures me: you are known.

I.M. *Philip Larkin*

Sorrow will keep its hour
surpassing all belief.
It will push through pavements, open
when it means to. It will fall
as acid rain corroding
bell-throats. Sorrow will slide
down gutters of fine print.
At dusk, a rushing whiteness,
will seize and hold you safe.

The Sun Descending

To the memory of Vera Cottew

I have the Oxford Blake you left me;
hold it as if to bring you close.
Walk with me where the old houses
offer their frogs and gnomes and artless
flower-filled swans made of bald tyres.
It will soon be night. The gutter's pouring
quicksilver and a broken bottle
glitters like Cinderella's slipper.

You loved the first of everything:
first breath of any season, first
light on anything, first blossom
on any bush, brush-stroke on canvas.

Half a lifetime, and I am holding
your favourite book, dark blue and gold.
Your spirit brushes mine. You walk
under the shining heavenly shell
with me, clean through the solid world.

Schrödinger's Cat Preaches to the Mice

To A.D. Hope

Silk-whispering of knife on stone,
due sacrifice, and my meat came.
Caressing whispers, then my own
choice among laps by leaping flame.

What shape is space? Space will put on
the shape of any cat. Know this:
my servant Schrödinger is gone
before me to prepare a place.

So worship me, the Chosen One
in the great thought-experiment.
As in a grave I will lie down
and wait for the Divine Event.

The lid will close. I will retire
from sight, curl up and say Amen
to Geiger counter, amplifier,
and a cylinder of HCN.

When will the Geiger counter feel
decay, its pulse be amplified
to a current that removes the seal
from the cylinder of cyanide?

Dead or alive? The case defies
all questions. Let the lid be locked.
Truth, from your little beady eyes,
is hidden. I will not be mocked.

Quantum mechanics has no place
for what's there without observation.
Classical physics cannot trace
spontaneous disintegration.

If the box holds a living cat
no scientist on earth can tell.
But I'll be waiting, sleek and fat.
Verily, all will not be well

if, to the peril of your souls,
you think me gone. Know that this house
is mine, that kittens by mouse-holes
wait, who have never seen a mouse.

Night and Dreams

I

'I come to you in a dream of ages
past,' sings Crab. He swirls his velvet-
seaweed cloak. 'When first we met,
and last, you will recall, I was
imprisoned in your father's house.'

Sea colours on his carapace,
wave-hiss, tide-rustle in his voice.
'Some fiend had tied my fearful claws –'
– Yes, I recall. I must have been
a skinny child of eight or nine

that night my father brought you home –
'No, let *me* tell,' says Crab, 'this is
my aria, *my* party piece.
Grandmother, mother, father, brother
and you, went to the local theatre

leaving me bound in parching darkness.
I prayed: Redeemer Crab, release me
by your own sidelong righteousness
from these straightforward evildoers.
Take me where my transparent children

float in their manifold sea vision.
Silence. Mouse-whisper, cockroach-scuffle.
I felt, not far, the Brisbane River
ebbing to salt creek, mangrove swamp,
and burst my bonds, O yes I did!

and raged through your dark house, and hid.
That night you dared not go to bed
finding me gone when you returned.
Splintered pencils and toys proclaimed
my ocean strength. How soon forgotten

what Stan and Olly did and said!
Time, time. I felt the tide returning
far off. O Salt Redeemer, come
(I prayed) let navies drown to feed me
with rotten stump, decaying belly,

or if I am to die, allow me
one crunchbone tender-balancing foot.'
– My father caught you. 'Ah, he did.
"We'll cook the brute tonight," he said.
"Bring me the hatpin." Someone put

a diamond eye on a steel stalk
into your father's hand to stab
my stalked eyes. O the blaze of pain
eclipsing light's immense mandala!
Seagreen, seablue, I raged to red.

Boiling, crab died. I became Crab.'

II

Crab is dressed for the feast: on lettuce shredded
to seaweed ribbons, cracked claws reassembled,
he lies among parsley curls and radish roses.
Our starchy Sunday-snowy cloth is set
with what remains of Greatgrandmother's china,
translucent white, rimmed with a deepsea blue.
On his great serving dish Crab's at the centre
of a splendid colour wheel: cucumber slices,
tomato, celery, carrot, egg: my work,
duly admired. My grandmother says grace.
'Where would you eat like this,' my father asks,
passing the homemade bread, 'except in Queensland?'
A lovely room. Windows give on the garden
rose and green panes of bubble-glass enchanting
the dullest day. The sideboard mirror offers
more light. Such light, restoring, recomposing
many who dined here. Most of them are dead.

III

'That's enough of pentameters,'
says Crab, returning to my dream.
– What shall I write, I ask. He writes,
so I won't miss his fearful joke:
THE DIRE BELLY VARIATIONS!

Making himself a cairn of stones
he says, 'This is my own rock group.
O I'm the original punk rocker
with a hatpin through my brain, my brain,
with a diamond hatpin through my brain.'

– Your jokes are awful. 'I know worse.'
– Impossible. 'Shall I rehearse
the names of those who've died from cancer?
O I'm the original merry prankster,
a diamond hatpin's all my eye.

Tell me, where are those who ate
my claws, my tender body meat?
Laurel and Hardy fans, long gone!
You cracked my hardware, ate my software.
Now I'm programmed in your brain.'

IV

More and more of the great questions,
such as: what am I doing here
in gumboots and a summer nightdress
in a moonlit garden chasing sheep?

The sheep are out. It's not a dream.
I'll mend the broken fence tomorrow.
What's left of night? Enough to dream in.
What dreams will come? Who else but Crab.

I ate him sixty years ago.
Ocean of memory, transposing
feaster and feast. He beckons, wearing
seaweed clothes, with sidelong charm.

'Shall we go to a pirate movie?'
– You like the sea? 'I like the bodies,
and "Take the lady below and make
her comfortable", that's what I like.

I can't be bothered with the love scenes.
I've opened hearts. I know what's in them.'
At interval he buys refreshments,
'Two seafood sticks. One without crab.

Come live with me and be my supper
where colours have no boundaries,
where every word is writ in water,
I'll put my arm around your waist.

I'll put my armour round your waist.
Shell after shell my soft self waxes.
Seek help! Sea kelp for drowning sailors.
Great questions all have wavering answers.'

Ghosts crowd to hear. O my lost loves.
Waking to hard-edge sunlit colours,
sharp birdsong, lamb-bleat, I recall
myself among the moonlit sheep

questioning – what? Why should I care
how long ago my death began?
Am I a ghost dreaming I'm human
with herbs to plant, a fence to mend?

Cups

They know us by our lips. They know the proverb
about the space between us. Many slip.
They are older than their flashy friends, the glasses.
They held cold water first, are named in scripture.

Most are gregarious. You'll often see them
nestled in snowy flocks on trestle tables
or perched on trolleys. Quite a few stay married
for life in their own home to the same saucer

and some are virgin brides of quietness
in a parlour cupboard, wearing gold and roses.
Handleless, chipped, some live on in the flour bin,
some with the poisons in the potting shed.

Shattered, they lie in flowerpot, flowerbed, fowlyard.
Fine earth in earth, they wait for resurrection.
Restored, unbreakable, they'll meet our lips
on some bright morning filled with lovingkindness.

1945

Nineteen forty-five. I have been sick
all the way from Brisbane; first time in the air.
My husband's waiting in civilian clothes.
Another name now. All those burning glances
cancelled, all those raging letters burned.
And my mocking friends – 'Holy MaTRIMony!'
'You've had your wings trimmed. You'll be Mother Goose.'

We melt with good old-fashioned happiness
at the desolate terminal. I see the city
ending in bush, St George's on the skyline,
KEENS CURRY on the hill. We find a cafe.
'Lunch is off. Afternoon tea's not on,'
the waitress snaps, and sniffs. She knows we're strangers.
Saturday afternoon. How doth the city

sit solitary. A shuttered delicatessen
proclaims HIGH GRADE AND CONTINENTAL FOODSTUFFS.
What continent? Perhaps they mean the mainland.
I'm in my summer clothes. A wind breathes cold
truth in those English trees that tried to fool me
with their false fronts on a tourist office poster.
Know'st thou the land wherein the citrons bloom?

I do. Exile's the name I give that knowledge.
Even as I say How Beautiful How Charming
why do I feel that some demonic presence
hovers where too much evil has been done
near the harmless rivulet, the Georgian buildings?
Hungry, we link our lives and wait for evening.
In my husband's luggage the *Tractatus* waits

with the world that was the case already fading.

Forty Years On

To Peter Bennie

I hear you are writing your memoirs,
old love. Are we all to go back
and inhabit the selves we abandoned
on Promenade Batter-My-Heart
and dance with our circle of lovers
in a strange resolution of distance?

We always turn first to the index
(speak truth!) to discover our name,
which now may be all we have left
of magical light and a body
untempered and whole. To be *there*,
and to feel the malicious delight

of naming the who-shall-be-nameless:
the White Russian who lived like an owl
undisturbed in a house of ill fame;
the curate who catechised boys
from his bathtub.
                              A madrigal-mixing
of alases and hey-nonny-nonnies:

young women who flocked to your smile
fell quiet. The war was over.
Our heroes returned and reclaimed us,
and life in the suburbs began
in earnest, however deadly.
Virtue was thick on the ground.

Come unto the index all you
who hankered for life everlasting
and only got life (which is endless,
as Wittgenstein says, in the way
that our visual field has no limit).
And the inward eye, too, without limit

looks away from the shuffle of autumn
and fills with perpetual summer:
a circle, and you among us
most loved of all, discoursing
on life and art, and no one
thinking of forty years on.

Sunset, Oyster Cove

To the memory of Edwin Tanner

I know better than to lie down
in sunshine in late afternoon
to drowse and wake at twilight with torturing midges
when those who know me so well
they could find me on any shore on earth
take for their breath the nightwind's: *Exile, exile.*

To all, to lovers, to friends
secure beyond falling out of love,
time brings at last their last time on earth together.
Let memory lie like sunlight
on this desolation of weeds.
            You are raked with pain, but alive, and paintings stand

            round the cave of your room; in the shadow
            of death, your death, they are binding
            your life to inviolate space.

                        For what do we grieve
if death is only an image
in the mirror of time's abyss,
the prior darkness when earth did not contain us?

How long, how late we would talk
of death, love, art, the enchanting
confusion of mortal questions. We could have talked
for a thousand years, and changed
our minds a thousand times,
like Goethe changing 'For all must melt away

to nothing,' after his friends
had it set in golden letters
for a scientific assembly.
                        I fear those dreams
when those I loved, now dead,
are speaking to those who died
in earlier times; they did not meet on earth

but smile, and know. They bid me:
restore, repair, remember.
Be with me here as you were, in pain but smiling,
here where the dying race
posed stiffly as grim dolls
for their last likeness, history closing round them.

As sunset paints neglected
damson and lively thistle,
and the tide returns to send the semaphore crabs
each to his burrow, flaunting
a pugilistic nipper,
affirm, 'No being can dissolve to nothing.'

Mid-Channel

*The days shall come upon you, that he will take you away with hooks,
and your posterity with fishhooks.*

Amos, IV, 2

Cod inert as an old boot,
tangling dance of the little shark,
perch nibble, flathead jerk –
blindfold I'd know them on my line.

Fugitive gleam on scale and fin,
lustrous eye, opalescent belly
dry and die in the undesired
element. A day will come,

matter-of-fact as knife and plate,
with death's hook in my jaw, and language
unspeakable, the line full out.
I'll tire you with my choking weight

old monster anchored in the void.
My God, you'll wonder what you've caught.
Land me in hell itself at last
I'll stab and swell your wounds with poison.

Not here, not now. Water's my kingdom
tonight, my line makes starspecks tremble.
The dinghy's decked with golden eyes
and still the cod boil round my bait.

Pastorals

To Desmond Cooper

I *Threshold*

Know that a peaceful harbour
framed by low hills, a refuge
that might be glimpsed one moment
in a happy dream, exists:
a marina spiky with masts;
salt glitter, boat-brightness rocking
in grey-green shallows, and gulls
reading in deeper sea-gleam
the text of wind and tide.

Some genius of earth
devised this generous place,
this charm of light compacting
sea, sky, the hills of Bruny,
the birds with airfilled bones,
the clouds like ghosts of sails,
into one form, one presence
whose guests we are, and welcome.
The ferry's engines throb

among water's ancient voices.
Children's and seabirds' cries
fade at the fringe of language
as the road leads gently upwards
to a gate where casuarinas
crosshatch the shining water.
The road leads on. But pause:
lift clear from time's refractions,
from the mind's reflective tricks,

this day; see its true shape.
Look how a lizard skims
from leaf-shade, and is basking
stone-still on stone, a finger-length

creature absorbing sunlight.
A crow with steel-bright eye
testing the pitch of silence
flaps to a neighbouring pine,
settles his dark voice down;

pause for a moment here.
These gums that fracture light
are home to the intricate compound
eyes of the insect kingdom,
and birds, whose eyes can read
the to-us-invisible pattern
of the polarised sky, are singing
what is real but still unnamed.
Our words and thoughts are polished

like pebbles ground in the stream
of time, but here's an enclave,
land held in arms of water,
where the plover and their young
are safe in feathery grasses
stirred by the seawind breathing
a prayer of peace and healing
in the pure, authentic speech
that earth alone can teach.

II *A Welcome: Flowers and Fowls*

Field of the cloth of gold!
Random as stars, the dandelions
crowd in their constellations.

A day of muted brightness
but for these blazing flowers
through which, at first by ones

and twos, then all at once,
a friendly host comes running.
Two beauties walk together,

Moorish princesses, distant
from the common flock; a few
are glossed in autumn colours,

bronze, sepia, russet brown.
All gather close and turn
their sharp archaic profiles –

You should have come with gifts
to us of ancient lineage.
We scratched the dust of Egypt.

Caesar carried us north.
We voyaged with Columbus.
I walk on, empty-handed

through taller reeds and grasses.
'O happy living things' –
as Coleridge says, the heart

must bless them, to be blessed.
And when at last I leave,
the flock, in benediction,

waits in the field of gold.
Seed of the seed of grasses
they fossick in will flourish.

Beyond the net of language
they know themselves immortal
as grassblade and grasshopper,

as the gods who fill their dishes.

III *Mt Mangana in the Distance*

The One, the Many: with or without
capital letters they remain
or change and pass through language, thought
and those half-apprehended moments
when strands of glittering atoms twine
together in one grand design.

An early Greek philosopher called
the triangle *first-born of beauty*:
first geometric form to hold
multeity in unity.
It does philosophy no harm
to settle for such angular charm.

Sharp tenderness of early spring:
let no abstraction crop the mind.
The wind that spoke of snow is gone.
Love-vine and running postman bring
promise of paradise regained.
The house, so long at home among

those creatures here by right, prepares
its gifts of foreign fruit and flowers,
holds welcoming windows to new light.
Old songs of earthly innocence
rise up on delicate beams of bone
as earth reframes her elegant

geometry, an earth so fluent
in mathematics she composes
skin, scale, fur, feather, leaf and petal
in cusp, curve, spiral, hexagon;
and for a loving eye encloses
one prospect in three planes of vision

the casuarinas' endless outlines
rough-sketched on foreground sky and water;
two distant arms of land dividing
distant water and sky, and last
the mountain, at the heart of distance,
a triangle of softest blue.

from BONE SCAN (1988)

IV *Arcady*

Mankind's ancestral dream:
one part of earth, one place
of elemental peace.
Fields, trees, a welcoming house;
water an eye reflecting
a calm world-spanning light
on hills the hand of time
smooths to a gradual curve;
shelter, refreshment set
for birds whose song was old
when history was new;
young trees planted to grow
among the pasture grasses
the Greek heroes walked through:
man's landscape goes with him.

From blue, green, bronze, grey, muted
by cloud-shadow, the mind
turns to a deeper colour
flourishing by the house:
part of ourselves, our books,
our elegies that summer
cannot be made to stay,
part of the breath sent sobbing
after lost presences,
the red rose with its legends
of beauty and desire
speaks of the skill unearthing,
from the common briar, a form
as bright as any dream.

V *Reflections*

Two worlds meet in the mirror
	of the quiet dam. The trees
lift stem and crown above
	their own calm images.

Rest, in the heart's dry season,
    where the green reeds stitch light
to light, where water levels
    unendingly the bright

ripple of leaf or wind-breath;
    inverts the bowl of sky
to a cup of deep enchantment,
    as if some perfect eye

saw memory and substance
    as one, and could restore
in depth, in flawless detail,
    time as it was before.

Why does the body harbour
    no memory of pain,
while a word, a name unspoken
    in the mind cuts to the bone?

When time is turned to anguish,
    lastborn of nature, rest,
where shade and water offer
    solace to all who thirst.

VI *Autumn Rain*

Chill rain: the end of autumn.
A day of sombre music,
a raindrop army drumming

to the plover's haunting cry.
Grief under a gold mask,
perhaps? More likely, joy

at the delicate abundance
stirring in sodden paddocks
to nourish generations

of spurred grey wings. A day
for the householder to listen
in peace to his tanks filling,

or watch the mushrooms making
themselves from almost nothing
in their chosen place, a domed

city among the pines;
but to any eye beneath them
dark suns with rays extending.

A day to think of death,
perhaps, or of children's children
inheriting the earth.

VII *Winter Afternoon*

A sun too mild to challenge
frost in the shady hollows
honours this afternoon
with light so sharp the gulls
a mile away flash silver.

Cold underfoot, how cold
the touch of air on hand
and face in lengthening shadows
by the dam's hoof-churned rim.
Explicit darkness stamps

and snorts. Two young bulls wheel
away, return and circle
like boys at play exploding
with aimless energy,
then stand stock-still, exhaling

a sour-sweet mash of grasses.
Clear light glosses their blackness:
taut flank, keel-curving breast,
bold eyeball, glistening muzzle
plumed with the warmth of breath.

No word that makes us mortal
touches their strength, or glints
on their serene horizon:
this winter's day, this field
where earth has set their table.

VIII *Sea Eagle*

Dusk, early springtime. Light's a tender
grey monotone, and silver-cold
water's a mirror where the slender
grasses in stony shallows hold
their shadows still. Twilight uncovers
old nightfall sorrows: friends and lovers
long lost, once beautiful. The hills
of Bruny darken. Darkness fills
thin ribs of water as the wading
herons stab at the edge of night.
Wingbeats: from a bare branch the white-
breasted sea eagle soars in fading
cloudlight. A late gleam from the west
catches him riding on a crest

of air to his untroubled gleaming
eminence. He turns and drifts,
his mile of quiet water seeming
a wingspan wide. How the heart lifts
from old hesperian sadness, follows
him homeward through the shadowy hollows
between the hills, accepting all:
the lordly hunter and the small
creatures who tremble at his rising.
Night voices wake as night comes on
and conjure when the last light's gone
the always known, always surprising
flight of the mind that soars to share
his pathway in cold shires of air.

IX Carapace

Hold in the hollow of your palm
this carapace so delicate
one breath would send it spinning down,
yet strong enough to bear the stress
of ebb, flow, metamorphosis
from skin to shell.

      Seasons have scoured
this beautiful abandoned house
from which are gone eyes, sinews, all
taken-for-granted gifts.
               I hold
in my unhoused continuing self
the memory that is wisdom's price
for what survives and grows beneath
old skies, old stars.

           Fresh mornings rim
the carapace of night with gold.
The sandgrains shine, the rockpools brim
with tides that bring and bear away
new healing images of day.

from *The Present Tense*
(1995)

Songs of Eve   I

I

Master of chaos, hold me close.
A voice clears darkness from pure space.

Fondle me. I am someone's name,
A form the world has never known.

A cracking dream. My bones are making,
one, and another. Light is breaking.

II

Cold sheets of colour, fingernail
of heavenly body, naked man,
clothed deity. And I begin
to know myself more beautiful

than all God's bright and simple shapes,
and feel the dews of passion ease
the lock of my unopened thighs,
see light possess earth's gentle slopes,

Adam's wide-open ribcage spring,
across a pulsing darkness, shut.
Bone of my bone, I know without
remembering, I speak your tongue.

III

Adam, what have you there?
It is a small bird, surely,
hatched out of God's blue breathing.
I feel it in my hand
trembling in warmth, and rising,
defying the grave earth
with its strange wings, grossly mounted.
My winged love, my soaring bliss.

IV

So this is the best
of all possible worlds.
His cleansing wit ordained it so:

the thrust and rapture
ordained to fall
back into ocean's shimmering witness.

The cock in full brilliance
crowing up morning,
body illumined and spirit touching

horizons alight
with a tinge of madness,
the afterglow of a lunatic moonset.

Eye to mind
in a raging welcome
we lie beyond the kingdom of darkness.

He leaves us alone
to paint our sensations,
our fairy tales, our fiery tales.

It is I, it is you,
in a crown of gold feathers
soaring and singing.

V

Angelo Draco, travelling salesman,
knocked at the door. Asked for my husband.

'Representing, *The Fruit of Knowledge*.
Think how the set would look on your shelf.

My product will help you to get ahead.
win scholarships, make the best of yourself.

Let me summarise, in case I've confused you,
we publish a yearbook every year.

Eight, ten, twenty years into the future
we'll still be in touch with you. Sign here.'

VI

Blood drop by blood
        drop by drop
                by drop
And the kingfisher takes me
        to his rank nest,
                warm food for his children.
In the smell of old fish and leaves and mould
a murderous demon not yet revealed
rejoices that God has wounded me.
Infants a handspan long are crawling
damnation-mad on the floor of hell.
Adam is hunting, his hounds are singing,
the deer is stricken. God creates nothing.
The world exists from eternity.

VII

I had no childhood, but
    my daughters will be children.

I have no mother, but
    my children will be daughters.

It needs no cosmic wrong,
    only the puzzled, growing
        wretchedness of one child,
            blind, whose friend says: 'Look!'

VIII
Adam as Black Minstrel, Eve as Mammy

Tarbaby, tarbaby, hush your cryin'
the stars are swarmin' the sunset's dyin'.

Hush your mouf, girl, spade's a spade.
I'm gonna get our firstborn laid.

Who's gonna lay him? Things is grim.
There's only me and you and him.

You want your boy to be a fairy?
Read your Bible Commentary:

Keep on readin' and shut your face.
We're all symbols of the human race.

Shine your shoes, boy, time to go
off to the whorehouse with Daddy-o.

Daddy I can't make it in this heathen place.
All of those whores have my Mammy's face.

IX
Tune: The House of the Rising Sun

All seasons through all centuries
      as mistress, whore and wife,
my body like a hollow reed
      has shaped the sound of life.

Philosophers and Saints have breathed
      their wisdom in my bed.
King David sleeps beside his harp.
      Great Solomon is dead.

My daughters grind the bones of kings
      in fields where armies bled
to nourish the immortal wheat
      to make their children's bread.

My soul dares to reveal itself
      now God himself is dead.
Old earth will give her yielding seed
      to see my daughters fed.

To Music

You of the Minute Waltz and the Four Seasons,
you of the earthen flute and grand piano,
you with your immortal numbers:
the Nine, the Thirty-Two, the Forty-Eight;
you of the infant trying out the pitch
of its few syllables, you of the birds,
of the first cuckoo in spring, the lark ascending
to carve its empire in a thousand notes;
you of Gaudeamus and Miserere,
music, fitting yourself to any language,
at home with love and death and revolution.
Music, made of the very air we breathe,
with us from everlasting, always new,
in throats, in guts, in horsehair and wooden bellies.
Sleeping for centuries in forgotten scores,
hiding in crumhorn, shawm, theorbo, sackbut,
rattling in the tambourine, rejoicing
at the horse and his rider flung into the sea,
silent by Babel's streams, hung on the willows,
loud in national anthems, marching with bagpipes,
jogging in headphones, waiting in lifts and buses,
lurking in telephones, raging in discos
everywhere
                nowhere without a human ear.

Midwinter Rainbow

I.M. Vincent Buckley

The immortal Signified
has deconstructed light.
Adonai Elohim,
I-am-that-I-am,
ineffable by name
and nature, hangs his sign
aloft for all to read.
How to deduce the rules
of his chromatic game?
Newton figured a path
for sunlight's deviation.
Save us from Newton's sleep,
said visionary Blake.
Read the scriptures and weep:
save us from one who makes
promises, promises
to Noah, that old soak,
and then, nine chapters on,
sits eating veal and cakes
prepared by Abraham's wife
before he torches Sodom,
just and unjust together.

I will be when and where
I will be, saith the Lord.
God, what a character!
Where could he set the rainbow
in that anterior age
when there was none to see it?

You laughed once when I told you
the luminous space between
inner and outer rainbows
is called Alexander's Band.

Wrap me in rags of time.
You are gone to the treasures
of darkness. I remain.
Some ancient presence writes
a soft-edged covenant
beyond interpretation
on the midwinter sky.

The Owl and the Pussycat Baudelaire Rock

You longed for night and the night is coming,
    the rays of the daystar fade and die,
the nightwind rises, the tide is waiting,
    and the years that are gone lean down from the sky.
    Baby my baby, I'll love you forever,
    when your head's burned out and your light's all gone,
    my eyes will find you in stony darkness.
    Baby my baby the night comes on.

Rock on, rock on till we reach that country
    where all is harmony and delight,
fragrance of amber, fathomless mirrors
    reflecting the gold and hyacinth light.
    Baby my baby I'll love you forever,
    when your brain's ground out and your dreams are gone
    I'll hunt you out through seas of darkness.
    Baby my baby the night comes on.

Rock on, rock on, my songs enfold you,
    the moon slides down and the water's wild,
the snowpeaks gleam on the far horizon,
    the sun will rise like a golden child.
    You asked for night and look it is falling
    your peace is here, your sorrow is gone,
    lie at my side in the rocking darkness.
    Baby my baby, the night comes on.

from *Collected Poems 1943–1995*
(Formerly uncollected poems)

The Dead Gums

Gigantic pillars bear the arching weight;
    They are the gums, dead, but their mighty roots
Hold still the silver branching weight aloft,
    Cold hearts from which no resurrection shoots.

They sound like trumpets' lightning through the soft
    Chiming of moonlight in the vaulted sky.
To me, awake or drowned in secret sleep,
    Though all the night is deaf beyond, they cry:

Know that the sickle-cutting sun will sweep
    And your leaves die like ours. A frosty sea
Will search your roots and wash away desire.
    Then death will seal the season's change, and we

Who light your heart now with our silver fire
    Will crack in the great storms, and be no more
Than a child's garden fenced with twigs, a frost
    Of shells crushed and bleaching on the shore.

Water-Music

Gently on the slipping stones
   moves the swift unfolding flood.
Ribbed with dusk, the stream intones
   requiem for restless blood.

All the overtones of day
   vanish in the sounding tide.
History dissolves away,
   I return to Adam's side.

Sleeping in a twisted root
   lies the subtle enemy,
still the bright and bitter fruit
   hangs untasted on the tree.

Empty, perfect swells the dream
   in its bubble-skin of sleep:
gathering upon the stream
   are the tears mankind will weep

when I bite the world apart,
   show the sweet corrosive core
and the sorrows at its heart
   salt their bread for evermore.

Last Meeting

Shadows grazing eastward melt
from their vast sun-driven flocks
into consubstantial dusk.
A snow wind flosses the bleak rocks,

strips from the gums their rags of bark,
and spins the coil of winter tight
round our last meeting as we walk
the littoral zone of day and night,

light's turncoat margin: rocks and trees
dissolve in nightfall-eddying waters;
tumbling whorls of cloud disclose
the cold eyes of the sea-god's daughters.

We tread the wrack of grass that once
a silver-bearded congregation
whispered about our foolish love.
Your voice in calm annunciation

from the dry eminence of thought
rings with astringent melancholy:
'Could hope recall, or wish prolong
the vanished violence of folly?

Minute by minute summer died;
time's horny skeletons have built
this reef on which our love lies wrecked.
Our hearts drown in their cardinal guilt.'

The world, said Ludwig Wittgenstein,
is everything that is the case.
– The warmth of human lips and thighs;
the lifeless cold of outer space;

this windy darkness; Scorpio
above, a watercourse of light;
the piercing absence of one face
withdrawn for ever from my sight.

'Can These Bones Live?'

Ezekiel 37.3

I

Rise up, you bones, wrap your foul rags about you.
All who lie rotten, rise, all whom earth nourished.
Gather, you living, for the death of earth.
The age of green is gone.
                  You dead kings rising,
look in vain for your kingdoms, earth is dying.
Children, gather and mourn, she leaves you nothing.
The foul wastes gather in her folds of brightness.
She is hacked and splintered. Cities breed like sores:
murderers, monsters, thieves, black marketeers.
All, all shall die. An evil peace will fall.
Time's music quickens for the dance of death.

II

Lovers, lie down and close your eyes.
You shall call up from stony ground
a shaft of green to catch the wind,
a wind to bring the cooling cloud,
a cloud to loose its waterdrops,
water to nourish springing green
to catch the wind to clear the cloud
so water wears the face of light.
Lovers, lie down and join your hands.
Your bodies answer light with light.

III

Earth turns from the fastness of night, wind stirs in peaceful spaces.
New grasses bandage her wounds, her scars grow velvety mosses.
Small creatures take their daily path through fallen cities.
On a glittering shore there lie, born again from curving sea-forms
a man and a woman, sea-wet, content in morning's brightness.
They bless the promise of sunrise, the dazzle of light on water,
sweet air, salt food, soft cloud, the flight of fearless sea-birds.
They welcome the holy sun, as water is robed in flame.
Bone to his bone they embrace, in the heart and substance of light.
The wilderness quickens with love. Earth knows them for her own.

The Speed of Light

To Rex Hobcroft

Out of the city's snarl of nerves
you bring me to this place I love
where distance and clear light dissolve
in space cleared by the sweep of wind
thoughts that inhabit weariness.
Beyond a pastoral landscape, hills
are flung like surf. Here one might speak
those dangerous words: *love, justice, good*;
bring from mind's prison its worst thoughts:
there's nothing that I might not lose,
and still affirm love, justice, good.

The undertow of landscape draws
mind and eye from their height. Waves run
through earth and break in the far light.
No traps, no contradictions wait
on calm horizons while the spirit
wakes between sleep and sleep to walk
the sweet-hued earth at ease, translate
landscape into a joy not known
through intellect: words, long outworn,
like desperate sentries hold us back.

Now with the speed of light joy fills
salt glitter and inland hills,
kindling pastures, the homes of men;
shadows falling for generations
in the same valleys, fields without shade;
free spirits in their cage of atoms.
Out of such joy the world was made.

Eloisa to Abelard

Solace and hope depart. God's finger traces
on fields of frozen darkness: You shall find
loss, absence, nothing. Walking on the wind
Our Lord speaks to a crowd of foolish faces,

no face that is not mine, while filtering through
gaps, honeycombs of memory you seem
but the faint ghost of a remembered dream.
Unveiled by pain, I bleed. My wound is you.

Lost in the well of space, my spirit hears
'Lucis creator optime...' The choir
entreats God, out of tune. I join my voice
to theirs. Nightfall's immense. I taste my tears.
I reap the harvest of my own desire.
No heart escapes the torment of its choice.

Abelard to Eloisa

Far above memory's landscape let the fears
unlatched from thundering valleys of your mind
carry their lightning. Stare the sun up. Find
kinetic heat to scorch your mist of tears.

All that your vision limned by night appears
loose in dismembering air: think yourself blind.
Louder than death in headlines the unkind
elements hawk my passion: stop your ears.

Deny me now. Be Doubting Thomas. Thrust
into my side the finger of your grief.
Tell me I am an apparition frayed
out of the tattered winding-sheet of lust.
Recall no ghost of love. Let no belief
summon me, fleshed and bleeding, from the shade.

Poet and Peasant

Where's the proud light of summer gone?
   – Spare me the old romantic pitch.
Autumn's last haemorrhage clots the lawn.
   – This rubbish makes my eardrums twitch.

Leaves fall, sands drift, long summers fade.
   – Well, mate, your troubles are your own.
Where is the world's great treasure laid?
   – For Christ's sake, leave the world alone.

What rakes your heart in the late night?
   – The wife's prolapse, the baby's cough.
I saw the gulls, pure flecks of light...
   – Take your poetic blinkers off.

... settle on the world-rounding sea.
   – You've had it, mate. Lay off the birds.
The spirit's hunger woke in me.
   – Since when was hunger filled by words?

Hear me, I'll lift your load of grief.
   – Then fix my ulcer, if you can.
I'll show you joys beyond belief.
   – No thank you. I'm an average man.

Frog Prince

The honeymoon went swimmingly.
She kissed him, glad that his touch was
cooler than cool. He asked the right
questions in the right tone of voice.
They danced all night beside the pool.

In bed she found him playfully
absurd. A year passed. Childless still,
she made a quilt embroidered with
her parents' coat of arms. He grew
stouter, suffered from warts, drank more.

Somehow the landscape changed in scale.
He strolled among the places where
water grew foul. A dripping fringe
of moss grew from the eaves. He swiped
at flies, and caught them on the wing.

One night something appalling flopped
on top of her. Her parents came
next day to visit, and found all
the ceilings weeping, their girl raped,
her mouth stuffed with a golden ball.

Emporium

Young Lady, what can I do for you?
Yes, of course, you want a lover.
We have this unrepeatable offer:
this beautiful model with floating hair.
Just look at the eyes! Of course it's tricky
to handle, the only one of its kind.
Think how your friends will envy you.

My dear young lady, back already?
So the model got out of control in the dark?
And the words he used when he chose to speak
didn't seem to suit your lovely home?
And your parents insist on trading him in?

Well, may I suggest our regular number,
our knitting-book type, as cool and smooth
as his cigarette, in Alpine drag,
germ-free, complete with sag-proof smile.

Good morning, Madam, yes I can guess,
you've settled down and you'd like a child.
They come in all kinds, you can take your pick.
This one won't give you a moment's worry:
all-girl, all-boy, yes, one of each,
good on their potties, pretty and clean,
obedient, socially well-adjusted.
What else could Madam possibly want?

Good morning, good morning, of course I remember.
If Madam was so dissatisfied
why did she not say so at the time?
Diseases, nightmares, obscure neuroses? –
Dear lady, those models were factory-clean
and we couldn't possibly trade them in.

But down in the basement we happen to have
that very old model with flashing eyes
(and hair still good!)... If Madam cares
to take it away she might possibly find
a part that could be used to fill
that gaping hole in Madam's heart.

Hyacinth

My sisters drowsed among the flowers
drunk with longing, drunk with love,
in their familiar mental moonlight,
dreaming fulfilment, fingers tearing
hymens of unopened buds.

The God came in his car
daily, snatched me away.
My sisters waited, silenced
by his appalling wealth.
Their pale flesh sickened him.
He scorned their gaping rapture.
We left them fluttering
hysterical white hands.

Life had no images
but those fixed in his eye.
We burned along the highways
in his outlandish car.
Earth, a pastoral dream;
Sea, membranes of colour.
Far off, the tarnished cities
glittered with abstract light.
Somehow our bodies solved
all physical equations,
keeping his pulsebeat hours.

Today I took the wheel
drunk with violence, drunk with love
Down, down through private horror
the bright disc spun towards me
matter and colour fused
the world in one explosion.

My head lolls on its stalk.
My sisters kneel beside me
stroking my hair and screaming
at the darkness on their fingers.

'"Wolfgang," said father Leopold'

'Wolfgang,' said father Leopold,
    take up your goose's quill.
Prepare to do as you are told.'
    The lad replied, 'I will.'

'OK, you little genius,'
    said Leopold, *con brio*.
'Write, for new ages to discuss,
    a ravishing string trio.

'Just jot it down, my brilliant son.
    I'll make you a fair copy.'
Wolfgang, too often dandled on
    archducal knees, got stroppy.

'Don't want to,' said the surly boy.
    'String trios make me sick.'
'Write it!' said Dad, 'or I'll employ
    Your well-known friend, The Stick.'

'Just keep your hairpiece on, old man,'
    said Music's favourite son.
Ruling his paper, he began
    (though muttering, 'Just the *one*)

to score the luminous tunes that flow
    undying through the heart.
My love, this only goes to show
    the mystery of art.

In Memoriam Sela Trau

I learned both what is secret and what is manifest,
for wisdom, the fashioner of all things, taught me.

Your word was always: *Peace*. Peace of the spirit,
a calm and luminous landscape of the soul
where peace was the clear atmosphere you breathed.

In this grim century of dispossession
you gave us your supreme possession, music.
Sela: your very name is linked with music,

as in the Psalms: a rest, an interlude,
a pause, without which music can't exist.
When the vibrations died, you'd hold your bow

briefly in utter stillness, so we listened
to that pure silence from which music grows.
Mother, musician, teacher, virtuoso

in the true sense of the word, from *virtus*,
strength, bravery, courage, virtue, excellence.
One of your pupils said that what she owed you

could never be repaid, except with life,
a life that showed what never could be spoken,
as music shows, if we have ears to hear it,

a wealth of life transcending speech and silence.
You spoke sometimes of all things linked together,
from starry space to flowers and all earth's creatures,

all one, both visible and invisible.
That perfect health and perfect peace might flourish
seemed possible to you, O pure of heart

to whom the tree of wisdom gave its shelter
in your long life. You counted as a blessing
that time you could not play your instrument

because of injury. 'A time to think
in quietness,' you said, 'about those things
I've had no time to think of.'

We think of you under the aspect of eternity
in springtime, when the earth is rich with blossom.
Your vision lights us. Sela, rest in peace.

Late Works

Time to think of your Late Works
in the pure daylit atmosphere
of mystical acceptance, freedom
from old monsters, etcetera.

Time to be calmly transcendental
and abstract, time to set the stakes
so high no one will bet on you,
fill any form with stuff that breaks

the form so everything pours out
in a Great Fugue no one can play.
All those you wanted to impress
are dead or sick or pretty crazy

and those you know will understand it
are not yet born. Nurse, I need paper.
No, not that kind, you idiot girl,
the kind you write on. Get me Matron,

Matron I need a fountain pen.
If you have any wits about you
they're PhDs requesting access
to things you can't remember writing

to people you don't now remember.
Time to make light of time. Forget it.
Look through it. Write those late great works.
What was it that you asked the nurse for?

No matter now. You have your life
before you, you're a child enjoying
your *self*, the unity of contrasts.
Whose hand is it that holds your pen?

Two poems by Alan Carvosso
(Uncollected)

O Sleep, why dost thou leave me?

For half an hour at least I kept
your image clear, a radiant portrait,
hoping to dream as usual
with all the virtuosity
of absent lovers. What is that

tune of Handel's, begging for
sleep's visionary joys? I see
your eye (what colour?) one sharp tooth
but not your smile, your simple solid
face. I read across my wall
late headlights' shorthand for a city
which harbours you, my wandering love.

Shadows thin to a faint stain.
I see the hard geometry
of furniture, a surface flush
of things waiting to fix me on
my rock. The early sparrows sharpen

their beaks. Over the gulf of sleep
your face and butter-coloured hair
balloon as if distorted in
a fun-house mirror. Come to me,
my earthy nymph, suffer my love
in sleep at last. What is that song?

On Wings of Song

Earth unlocks wings, flowers, leaves, old jewels of sunlight.
In murmuring crowds the Sunday pilgrims throng
to a summer concert in the public gardens.
Blue air walks between lime and elder, singing,
as the band begins to play 'On Wings of Song'.

Under the English trees still thick with summer
two lovers walk; no longer young, they see
yellow invade the pure, harsh green of lime trees,
and breathe as with a single inspiration
the riches of late flowers. Light's clarity

can spare them nothing. Faces are more abstract,
flesh wears the gravity that pulls it down.
Each sees a flawless other still, erasing
years, years, when absence simplified to anguish
kept them awkward and truthful, in their own

prisons of memory drinking the sublime
love-fire of *this must be*. At last, though late,
they stroll upon green-mantled graves, abandoning
as it were leaf by leaf their lofty anguish,
content to pass unnoticed here, to wait

and learn what time will tell. Uprooted headstones
lean upon flowering vines. The lovers read
what time has told, flaking memorials:

The First White Child sleeps in its charnel cradle,
many lovers are dead, and dead indeed.

Round them, enmeshed in change, a city alters.
New buildings fit in holes ripped overhead
by steel and glass, but here the lovers, carried
on wings of song, rest in a blossoming garden
at peace, one evening closer to the end.

Fyfield*Books*

Two millennia of essential classics
The extensive Fyfield*Books* list includes

Djuna Barnes *The Book of Repulsive Women and other poems*
edited by Rebecca Loncraine

Elizabeth Barrett Browning *Selected Poems* edited by Malcolm Hicks

Charles Baudelaire *Complete Poems in French and English*
translated by Walter Martin

The Brontë Sisters *Selected Poems*
edited by Stevie Davies

Lewis Carroll *Selected Poems*
edited by Keith Silver

Thomas Chatterton *Selected Poems*
edited by Grevel Lindop

John Clare *By Himself*
edited by Eric Robinson and David Powell

Samuel Taylor Coleridge *Selected Poetry* edited by William Empson and David Pirie

John Donne *Selected Letters*
edited by P.M. Oliver

Oliver Goldsmith *Selected Writings*
edited by John Lucas

Victor Hugo *Selected Poetry in French and English*
translated by Steven Monte

Wyndham Lewis *Collected Poems and Plays* edited by Alan Munton

Charles Lamb *Selected Writings*
edited by J.E. Morpurgo

Ben Jonson *Epigrams and The Forest*
edited by Richard Dutton

Giacomo Leopardi *The Canti with a selection of his prose*
translated by J.G. Nichols

Andrew Marvell *Selected Poems*
edited by Bill Hutchings

Charlotte Mew *Collected Poems and Selected Prose*
edited by Val Warner

Michelangelo *Sonnets*
translated by Elizabeth Jennings, introduction by Michael Ayrton

William Morris *Selected Poems*
edited by Peter Faulkner

Ovid *Amores*
translated by Tom Bishop

Edgar Allan Poe *Poems and Essays on Poetry*
edited by C.H. Sisson

Restoration Bawdy
edited by John Adlard

Rainer Maria Rilke *Sonnets to Orpheus and Letters to a Young Poet*
translated by Stephen Cohn

Christina Rossetti *Selected Poems*
edited by C.H. Sisson

Sir Walter Scott *Selected Poems*
edited by James Reed

Sir Philip Sidney *Selected Writings*
edited by Richard Dutton

Henry Howard, Earl of Surrey *Selected Poems*
edited by Dennis Keene

Algernon Charles Swinburne *Selected Poems*
edited by L.M. Findlay

Oscar Wilde *Selected Poems*
edited by Malcolm Hicks

Sir Thomas Wyatt *Selected Poems*
edited by Hardiman Scott

For more information, including a full list of Fyfield*Books* and a contents list for each title, and details of how to order the books, visit the Carcanet website at www.carcanet.co.uk or email info@carcanet.co.uk